up HILL down DALE

Travelogues By

Asis Mukherjee

BlueRose ONE.com
Stories Matter

First Published in November 2022

ISBN: 978-93-5704-068-6

BLUEROSE PUBLISHERS

www.BlueRoseONE.com

info@bluerosepublishers.com

+91 8882 898 898

Cover Design:

Aveek

Typographic Design:

Rohit

Distributed by: BlueRose, Amazon, Flipkart

The Book Dedicated to

Shyamali Mukherjee.

Contents

Sandakphu-2017

A silver flash in the summer sky,
An aeroplane is passing by.
An old man and four young guys,
Heard the call of the mountain high.
They took a flight to the northern sky,
And landed beyond the plane not so high.
Chances may not come twice again,
So they took an age-old Jeep on hire,
Heading for the mountain and bon-fire!
Arriving at the forest rest house at Gairibus,
They called it a day responding the call of a wild thrush.
Next day morning leisurely,
They drove for Sandakphu pleasurely.
Snow beaten track soft and white,
Above azure sky not a sign of kite.
Chirping birds here and there,
Sandakphu welcomed with chilled beer!
That lazy, hazy, crazy day of strolling around,
Their ecsatasy knew no bound.
Next day they woke up before the morning chime,
To behold the "Sleeping Buddha" wake up in the first sunshine.
And they stood perplexed for a while or endless time!

*****

Up hill, down dale

Asis Mukherjee

It was late May and the just right season for a flight to the hill, when we arrived in Jorethung, a small town in the West Sikkim, situated at the confluence of the rivers Rammam and Rangeet. A four hour bus ride following the course of Rammam river via Sombaria, took us through the picturesque valley of Daramdin to Ribdi(8000 feet), a reomote village in southwest Sikkim perched on the slope of a hill. Visible through the forest on the opposite hill, was the Rammam Trekkers' Lodge and the trek route to Phalut. The only bus that could take us there would leave the following morning. We put up, therefore, at a local house and the cool mountain air soothed our spirit along with our aching muscles.

The following morning we were on the trail that lead to Versey(10100 feet), a nine kilometer trek from Ribdi via Hiley. The forest rest house at Hiley provided us with tea and a splendid view of the Kanchendzonga.

We resumed our journey along a path that cut through a dense forest of silver fir, hemlock and magnolia with rhododendrons creating a riot of colours here and there to liven up the route. Pinpoints of sunlight stole in through the leafy canopy of the branches overhead to trace patterns across our path. But as so often happens in the hills, a heavy downpour overtook us soon and drenched to the skin, we sought shelter in a lodge. Aptly christened Guraskunj, the Nepalese term for rhododendron resort, it had been built on the summit of a hill, from where a small number of trek routes led off in different directions, including one to Chiwabhanjang on the Singalila Range.

The two days we spent at Guraskunj, seemed to represent an idylic period, surrounded as we were by an abundance of orchid and rhododendrons. The following dawn had yet another delight in the store for us. The veil of cloud that had been obscuring the face of Mt. Kanchendzonga, gently driffted off, revealing the entire range in all its glory. With memories of that spectacular view still lingering in our minds, we left for Ribdi.

The following morning we undertook the nine kilometer trek to Gorkey, famed for its natural beauty. It involved crossing the Rammam River, the demarcation line between the states of Sikkim and West Bengal.

From Gorkey in Darjeeling district we made our way to Rammam a three hour trek through dense forest. It rained all the way and by the time we reached the well-furnished Rammam Trekkers'Lodge, we were exhausted. As we warmed ourselves by the fire, the sun emerged from behind its cloud cover, lighting up the village, the forest, the distant hills on the horizon and the valleys below.

Setting out the following morning, we passed through Rammam village on our way to Srikhola. At the Srikhola Trekkers' Lodge located on the banks of Srikhola River, we were given the alarming news that a strike had been called in the district by the rulling political party and no transport would be available for the return journey, should we fail to start out immidiately. Without waisting a moment, therefore, we left for Rimbik to catch the bus to Darjeeling town, from where we would make our way to Siliguri. Within a couple of days we were back in Calcutta - anticlimactic end to an exhilarating experience.

*****

Straight from the heart

Asis Mukherjee

As I panted and sweated my way up, the rucksack on my back felt heavy as a rock. The mild October shunshine lent, however a soothing touch. The view of the bridge over the river Alakananda came into focus and the town of Joshimath appeared on the opposite bank, as I gained altitude. A two hour trek brought me to a village. The first house I approached belonged to the village chief tain and his absence made no difference to the warmth of the welcome accorded by his young wife and daughter by a perfect stranger like me.

Relaxing in their courtyard after lunch , I gazed at the Alakananda flowing past , the ripples on its surface glittering in the sun. And I recalled how I had set out for Kagbhusundi Tal near Ratban Peak in the Garhwal region, putting up at the gurdwara in Govindghat, the starting point of the valley of Flowers and Hemkund Sahib. The place had been as disolate as a haunted house, with nary a visitor in sight. The residents of the upper settlement , I was told, had already moved to lower altitudes for the winter. Getting a porter to accompany me would, I realised, be next to impossible. The only option I had was to change my route.

The following morning, I was on the new route to the Chenup Valley. A Rishikesh- bound bus, starting from Badrinath, had taken me from Govindghat to the new bridge over the Alakananda, the starting point of my trek to the largely unexplored valley.

Here I now was, in this unknown village, with little information about the place apart from the name of my absent host, Bagicha

Singh who soon turned up and greeted me as though we were old friends. It was here that the positive side of human nature acquired for me, the cynical city dweller, a whole new dimension.

Equipped with a great deal of useful information, I set off, the next day, for Rampur (popularly known as Thang), the last village on this route, lying at the end of a three- hour trek. And a picturesque little place it was too, clinging to the green slope of a mountain. Accustomed by now to the hospitality of hill people, I did not hesitate to make myself comfortable at the home of Bagicha's brother.

The later was out, but soon returned with a bundle of wood he had been out collecting. The robust young fellow made me a cup of tea and gladly accepted the biscuits I offered him from my stock of rations. We took a stroll around the village in the evening and during dinner which he prepared and served, we chalked out our plans for the following day.

We set off right after breakfast, carrying only the bag containing my camera and walking at a brisk pace, because we planned to cover in a day a distance that usually took trekkers 48 hours to traverse. The main reason for our haste was to avoid a night's halt in the valley, not the most desirable of experinces in late autumn.

As we gained height, the village fell away, looking like a picture postcard in the distance. To the east emerged the twin peaks - Hati and Ghori - the aptly named after the animals they resembled in shape. The Nandadevi towered over the other peaks in the famous circle of mountains to the south-east.

A trek of three hours brought us to the shoulder of the ridge we were heading for and we stopped for a well-deserved break. Lingering over our packed lunch, we drank tea prepared by my friend and allowed ourselves a leasurely smoke.

Which was just as well. For the last leg of ascent was so tough that I could not only had to hand over my camera bag to my companion, but was forced to take his help in scaling the bare surface of the sharp gradient. Hands and feet scrabbling for a hold, I finally managed to make it to a spot where I could stand erect and play the monarch of all I surveyed.

From this point, the valley stretched away to the north, from where a stream lay frozen in motion. Looking down, I was overcome by vertigo. Ahead, beyond Joshimath, stood the "beastly" duo, Hati and Ghori. Both the east and west summits of the Nandadevi were clearly visible in the distance.

The prelude to winter had turned grass and the juniper bushes a reddish brown. The trail to Sonasinker, a local pilgrimage spot, stretched to the north. My carefree explorations of the area were nipped in the bud by my companion's warning that we were encroaching on the habitat of wild bears. I stopped in my tracks, noticing, for the first time, the large scythe he was carrying, ovbiously for self-defense. Within an hour, we were on our way back, spurred on, no doubt, by the need to avoid close encounters of the wild kind!

Within 24 hours, I was bidding goodbye to my friend, host and guide who had managed, within a brief span of time, to carve for himself a permanent niche in my heart. As I reached the bridge over the Alakananda and boarded a Haridwar- bound bus heading for the foothills, my thoughts continues to dwell on the people of this region who lent the concept of human kindness a new dimension and made every journey into the unknown an enriching experience.

*****

Just another day in paradise

Asis Mukherjee

A smooth drive of three hours and a half through Mahananda Sanctuary took us from New Jalpaiguri Station to Jorethung a pivotal town of West Sikkim. A small lunch break at a moderate restaurant; meanwhile we managed to book our seats in the commander service jeep bound for Utterey, a small hamlet in the West Sikkim. After having our lunch we, a four member team from Kolkata, occupied our seats and the jeep started at about 1-30 p.m. for Utterey. Though in bengali the name signifies a point in the north but actually the small village situates at the farthest point of West Sikkim bordering Nepal.

In the tourist map of Sikkim this place has not yet gained any status of so-called tourist spot like Gangtok, Yumthang or Pelling. In fact, Pelling has now become overthronged by hotels and you may come across familiar face while staying there during peak season. Moreover the crowd of tourists sometimes seems to break the tranquility of the mountain. And that is main reason which drove us to a new place in the familiar hill for peace and solace of mind for a couple of days.

So for the next four hours we drove through the hills and dales along the course of "Little Rangeet" towards it's upper valley. We left behind the confluence of "Rangeet" and "Rammam" at Jorethung. After more than a couple of hours non-stop drive we arrived at "Sinshore Bridge", a long spectacular suspension bridge on "Sinshore Khola" and named after it. It is one of the highest suspension bridge in Asia and famous tourist spot as well. Tourists from Pelling thronged around on local sight seeing. We crossed the bridge and drove further five kilometers. Our jeep stopped at the doorstep of "Green Valley Resort". As we checked in the hotel, evening set in the valley.

The morning wore a bright sunny face and we woke up at starting sound of the service-jeeps. This is the only throb of life we faced here. After the three service jeeps left for their different destinations, the valley again slipped into silence. Opposite to our hotel a lonely young shopkeeper went on playing his guitar and singing all by himself in front of his shop kept open. Only a few passersby stopped for a while perhaps attracted by his music. A beautiful scene that would remind you "The Solitary Reaper" of William Wordsworth. The only motorable road proceeds further towards the West. The river is not visible from this point, however if you walk a few yards up or down hill you will hear it's rumbling sound from below the gorge. The valley is stretched towards south and there , at the far end of the cultivable field, where the wall of the hill rises erect , stands a beautiful temple of Goddess Durga. On the hill top there is a small Gompha. An easy concrete foot track would take you at the hill top. We passed the day leasurely just strolling around. Though everybody around was engaged in brisk businesses of life, silence reigned supreme in the whole valley.

During the dead hours of the next day we set out for Chitre along the upstream of the "Little Rangeet". It was around four to five hours trek uphill towards Chiwabhanjan depending upon your stamina and load on your back. Towards the end of the village approximately half a mile from the hotel we came across a "Trout Breading Centre" of the Fisheries Department. Our foot track came to the river-bed and we could see the stretch of green cultivated field and beautiful houses on the other bank of the river. Gradually we entered through cardamom bush into the deep of the woods and as we marched forward the forest became more and more dense. The river was flowing down by the side of our trail. Sometimes we caught a glimpse of it; sometimes we could hear its music. Huge trees of a wide varieties engulfed us. Everywhere it was moistened and faint sunbeams filtered through the leafy canopy overhead. We walked together because of the fear of wild bear. After four hours of continuous trek we came to an open space amidst the dense forest. The forest bunglow of "Chitre" stood like a picture postcard at the far end. Deep green ridges encircled the area giving it a shape of bowl. The rest house, completely made of wood, was a piece of unique craftsmanship. The whole area was disolate and quiet. A few yaks we're grazing nearby. Apart from that there was no sign of movement. The gurgling sound of the stream that formed the "Little Rangeet" was heard but the stream was not visible. We stepped in the balcony and found the doors of the bunglow locked. The entire melieu would create an uncanny feeling in you as depicted in "The Listeners" by Walter De La Mare. Yet you would be bound to fall in love of this place and could hardly resist the desire to spend a moonlit night in this forest rest house.

But alas! We were bound to retreat. After an hour's rest and having consumed our packed lunch and coffee we resumed our return journey for Utterey. Chiwabhanjan is an hour's trek uphill from this point. But our route had now become familiar. We began to descend down and down along the course of the "Little Rangeet". We observed that two streams from Chiwabhanjan range formed the beautiful river. The sign of the village appeared when the clock struck 4-30 p.m. The last leg of our trek seemed to be endless but at length we came back to our lodge with leaden feet. It is advisable to spend a night at Chitre. Next day morning we bade good bye to this paradise and left for Pelling. That is a familiar place; a familiar story. But our longing for staying just another day in Paradise remained for ever vibrant in our hearts.

*****

The pilgrim's progress

Asis Mukherjee

"PANWALIKANTHA" --- Sometimes it's the name that draws our first attention without any reason. So when I got acquainted with the place in anarticle, the appeal was irresistible to me to visit it ,which is situated on the old pilgrimage route in the Central Garwal. Shortly we two; myself and Pradeep Biswas, set out for Tehri via Haridwar. Tehri was the ancient capital of Garhwal on the bank of Bhagirathi, but now it has lost his glamour and importance.

We left it behind and took the road to Ghuttu along the upstream of Bhilangana, a tributary of Bhagirathi. By late afternoon our only bus stopped at the road- ahead of the village Ghuttu which spread on the eitherside of the beautiful little river Bhilangana. It was a quiet hamlet in the lapof the Himalaya on the bank of a rivulet which was cascading down with the crystal blue water from khatling glacier and ghusing down to pour its water into the Bhagirathi.

We checked in the forest-rest-house. Putting our belongings in the room we set out again for a stroll around the village with an eye to searching twoporters for our next few days trek. We walked down to the riverbed and sitting on a flat stoneslab unleashed ourselves into the tranquility of the place against the setting sun. The rivulet flowed us to the past when the pilgrims and saints used to travel and halt on their pilgrimage along this route from Bhagirathi Valley to Mandakini Valley. Presently this roadhead village Ghuttu offers a number of treks including Shahasratal, Khatling Glacier and Kedarnath via masartal etc. You can get your provisions and porters and guides for your requirement here.

We engaged two local men as our porters and when we came to know from them that approaching for Khatling Glacier wouldn't be judicious in this early summer on account of heavy accumulation of snow in the uphillahead, we changed our mind instantly for 'Panwali Kanta' which was our primary objective. So we told them likewise and returned our nest. In the early morning the two porters peeped in and awakened us with two glasses of tea. I counted it as an indication of their sincerity which provedvery helpful later. We got up and prepared as they were busy on repackingtheir loads. We left our Nightshelter at about 6.30 in the morning and crossing the Bhilgana on foot bridge came on the left bank and immediately began to climb throuh the zigzag village foot-track. The village, the river, the foot-track to Gangi all remained picturesquely in shilhoutte assunshine was yet to appear in the valley below crossing the high ridge of the mountain. As we gained altitude we were getting warmer under the morning sunlight, though cool bridge often soothed us as frequently as we paused for a breath. Kanta is the colloquial term of a ridge. But Panwali Kanta is not only a ridge. it is a watershed between the two valleys of the Bhagirathi and the Mandakini rivers as well as it is also lucrative to the local 'gurjars' or the shepherds for its vast pasture of grassland around. During summer they used to settle here with their heards and continue to stay until winter falls. The Height is about 12000 feet above sea level and this place naturally offers a magnificent view of the peaks of the central Himalaya of the Gangotri region.

After a continuous march of three hours and half on the bare slope of themountain, Tirpan Singh, the guidde-cum-porter of our team declared a teabreak. This was well deserving. He lit a small fire and prepared the liquor within a few minutes. It rejuvenated our energy and we resumed our journey. Tirpan proposed me to reach Panwali the same day which meant to cover up a distance of two days march. It is about 16 kilometres andthe gain of altitude is 6000 feet.

Nevertheless it's labourious but the track was well defined and good. We now noticed big trees in abundance and we halted in the shed for our lunchas the sun crossed the midday.

In the afternoon we found a thached shop in the middle of the forest to myutter surprise and entered for a cup of tea. Tirpan informed me that a localvillager ran this seasonal multipurpose shop for those Gurjars of the up hillpasturage. Here we came across a Bengali sadhu to whom we offered a cup of tea. We came to know that his partner left him behind and he decided to spend the night here. We hurriedly finished our cups and rushed for the last leg of our's days March. While going through the forest Tirpan showed us some hideouts which the local poachers used to kill 'bharals' and deers by shotgun.

During late afternoon we came above the tree-line and soon we crossed thefinal ridge where from we caught the glimpse of the Majestic Himalayan range in the horizon and in front of us laid out a vast grasay pasture -- that's'Panwali Kanta' , our destination. We unleashed our rucksack from our backand laid down flat on the carpet of the nature utterlyfatigued. When, after - 'a-while, we could manage to drag us into the two storied mudhouse of the Panwali dharamshala we were greeted by Tirpan with mug full of steamingtea and plate full of snacks. He took our rucksacks in the upper room whilewe sat at the doorstep with our tea. When the goal was achieved, only tranquility prevailed, which we could feel all around. As the sun set, the peaks of Gangotri region in front visible from this part including Rudragayara and Khatling which I could recognise, began to change its colour to bid adieu to the setting sun. The vastness of the land, where we stood upon, the greatness of the mountain encircled us and the calmness of the surroundings entered into our soul awakenin a reverential feeling in the mind. We stood perplexed till darkness engulfed the surrounding and star studded canopy was hovered in the sky. A piercing cold wind drove us back to our nest.

We came across, to my utter dismay, the counterpart of that Bengali Sadhu who was left behind enroute. I didn't like to interact with him but Pradip collected a lot of information about them. As he told me, both of them fled from their home in the mofussil of Bengal in want and were roaming about in disguise of saints from the Gangasagar. What disgusted me most was their deceitful appearance by dint of which they lived a better life than what they did before. Moreover they didn't think for their families and children whom they left behind selfishly.

Morning wore a bright Sunny face and as we came out our hearts filled withecstasy. The weather was pleasant and the sign of life of a few Gurjar families around there and their herds awakened in the prevailing tranquility. There was no hurry-skurry. Life here rolls on along with the sun. After a lightbreakfast we picked up our rucksacks and bade goodbye to those local people who gave us shelter yesternight and stepped out on the track that led to 'Triyuginarayan' via 'Khunta Khal' the local name of a moderate passlying a few kilometres ahead.

But soon we came to a halt as we found our porters were waiting there for us. Everything around was shining but the face of Tirpan Singh, our guide, whose wrinkled forehead bore some serious indication. "What happened?"when asked, he simply showed me the foot track in front which had been buried under the deep snow and it's next to impossible to locate it and follow the same. The only alternative, as he suggested, if we wanted to proceed further, was to climb the cliff and to walk along its razor's edge untill 'Khunta Khal' appeared on our way. Obviously his suggestion put ourcourage and conviction to an acid-test, because it would be a risky attemptto trek on the sharp edge of a ridge without any support of 'lifeline', the rope, which could resist any unwanted fall or acccident. Nevertheless, we decided to proceed.

So we left the usual track and began to scale the slope of the ridge using allof our four limbs. Tirpan was leading followed by myself and next to me Pradeep and after him the porter all with their own load. As I came upon thetop of the ridge, I paused for a while, feeling the intensity of the wind and noticed the sharp fall of about one thousand feet on the other side where no snow could even accumulate. I poised my balance and concentration, then followed the foot steps left behind by Tirpan who already crossed the riskprone zone and waited for my arrival. I traversed the razor's edge safely and anchored beside him. Now only I could get time to look behind and anxiously noticed that my both behinders tried to cross that formidable ridge but they sank down on their knees. I immediately sent Tirpan, who was also watching them and finally he managed to fetch them safe one byone with great craftsmanship and courage.

The Ridge became flattened and we felt comfortable and safe and resumedour walk ahead in a row as usual through kneedeep snow. But 'Khunta Khal'or the pass was still a long-way. While plodding through the soft snow I hoped that after crossing the pass this hazardous journey might come to an end. Tirpan brought to our notice the pagmark of a Himalayan Bear on the soft snow which thrilled all of us. We paused en-route to "Khunta Khal"where Tirpan showed us the remains of a group of poor pilgrims who wereburried under and an avalanche last year. But all thesecould not stir our mind to a great extent because we were too embarrassed with the condition of the snow which now and then reached our west level. Ultimately we came upon the pass and with utter dismay noticed the terrible condition of the age-old foot track completely burried under snowand beyond negotiable condition.

So as Tirpan begin to descend the slope through the thick bush and hedgeleaving the foot-track aside, we came to his heel with leaden feet.He already noticed a shaphered's hut at the bottom of the slope amidst a small green pasture of land and selected it as our night's shelter and whenwe all reached there he broke off the day

In no time we rearranged the lonely hut and composed ourselves with our mattrasses and sleeping bags laid out while the porters brought a huge log and lit a fire. With steaming mugs of tea and snacks we soon recovered ourenergy which was drained out to the buttom in last eight hours of prolonged march through soft snow at about twelve thousand feet above sea level. There was no human being in the vicinity though 'Mogguchatti' was only a few kilometres further. The starry night-sky was visible through the perforated thatched roof of the hut and we rolled down in the womb of our sleeping bags after early dinner.

The following morning, as we left for 'Soneprayag', the roadhead on the Kedarnath route, a heavy downpour accompanied us till Triyuginarayan where we halted for a while. Though drenched to the buttom we visited thetemple where the holy marriage of Lord Shiva and Parvati took place underthe priesthood of Lord Vishnu according to mythology. Once important pilgrimage has now lost its importance to the modern travellers of Kedarnath who normally have very little time in their tight-scheduled package-tour to visit this beautiful place and the temple. It seemed to methat the temple along with a few habitats around remained in the hoary past with the ever-burning holy-fire as an evidence of the great marriage.

We also added some wood to the fire and prayed to the holy couple and headed for a hotel in the usual life of din and bustle of our world.

*****

Step by step towards the Hill

Asis Mukherjee

When autumn breeze starts blowing and the sky turns azure and clouds like combed cotton sway, I can hear the call of the Himalaya to my inner ear every year. It almost bends me to pack up and set out for the hill responding it's becon. That year also I set out for a sojourn to Sikkim, our neighbouring state abundant with lustrous beauty of nature, accompanied by my colleague turned friend P. K. Deb. The North Bengal bound train brought us to New Jalpaiguri Station in a sunny morning and we headed for "SNT" bus stand at Siliguri. After a brief pause for tea and snacks, we set out for Rabongla, a small but calm and clean town in the South Sikkim District.

Our bus took around four hours to reach Rabongla via Jorethung and Namchi. We alighted from the bus and checked in a nearby hotel. Rabongla is a small town very clean and quiet opposite to the towering Maenam hill. Occupying our room in the hotel and having our lunch we two set out for a stroll around the town and then we came across another group of four mountain lovers from Konnagar and Uttarpara who came and put up in the same hotel an hour before we reached. They also came with an eye to exploring the Maenam hill and surroundings. So we easily tied up with friendship and marching together revised our plan for the next day. After a brief stroll around we came back to our hotel and all sat down in the lounge with coffee. We checked our ration for the next day and after distribution packed it. After that we spent a nice evening in gossiping and exchanging our experiences until dinner. We went to our rooms after dinner at about nine p.m.

Next day morning we woke up early as usual and packed up our rucksacks and assembled at the lounge of the hotel. While having our breakfast we ordered packed lunch for us. We set out around nine in the morning and soon we took a zigzag foot track leading towards Meanam hill. It's a reserved forest around thirty seven square kilometers and the height of the hill is twelve thous itand five hundred feet above sea level. As we gained altitude the forest became dense. Varieties of trees and hurbs are in abundant for nature lovers and botanists. After a couple of hours trek we saw a watch tower amidst the jungle. We paused for a while for rest. We climbed the tower and watched around. Someone of us proposed to spend the night over there. But we so far crossed only half of the way so the proposal was immidiately turned down and we resumed our march. We already gathered information that there's a little monestery at the top of the hill. After four hours and a half we covered a distance of twelve kilometers and reached the top of the hill where we discovered a disolate monestery amidst the dense forest. The surrounding was clear and two rooms of the monestery was shut but not locked. So we easily occupied the front room and rearranged our belongings and came outside with our packed lunch to devour it and rejuvenate our fatigued body. Afterwards so long the daylight prevailed we explored the surrounding and all of a sudden we discovered the "Bhaledunga", the famous cliff where from the "Tista" river could be seen flowing far below the gorge. The height of the cliff from the river bed was around five thousand feet and the view was breathtaking. Before dark we returned our temporary nest. As evening fell the entire jungle sank into deep darkness of the night. Only the canopy of the starry sky was visible. We lit a small fire fortea and warmth also. Encircling the 'bon fire' with steaming tea mug in hand we absorbed in chatting and singing. Beyond our vibrant presence amidst the dense forest there was no sign of life. We were trying our best to break the silence and darkness around us but in vain. So after two rounds of tea perpetually, we set to prepare noodles for our dinner. We finished our dinner and slipped into sleeping bags at around seven thirty in the evening which seemed too early in our usual city life. But due to tiredness we soon lost in to sleep. Next morning we woke up too early and instead of morning tea or breakfast we packed up hastily and began to discend at rapid pace. We rushed back to our hotel at Rabongla in less than two hours. We ordered for tea and breakfast and refreshed ourselves.

After a brief pause we took the service jeep bound for Namchi. At Damthang we alighted from the jeep and the jeep took a turn and disappeared. Damthang is a small village at the foot of Tandong hill. Before starting for our new destination, we assembled before a multipurpose shop and ordered for tea. Meanwhile were trying to gather some information of the Tandong forest and the Gompha. An old man sitting in front of was also watching us and he suggested to wrap our feet with tobacco leaves to get rid of leaches in the forest. We were, indeed, not prepared for this. We expressed our thanks and bought some tobacco leaves from the nearby shop and wrapped it on our foot. We bought some rice and packets of biscuits and sugar for our tea and lunch. It's one hour and a half trek through the reserve forest of Tandong to reach the top of the hill. So we finished our tea and started for our new destination leasurely. As we entered into the forest varieties of trees and bushes engulfed us. The trunks and branches of the trees were heavily festooned with clinging beard like moss. Yarning for sunlight vines clambered up the tree trunks. Gigantic ferns took the shape of garden umbrellas. Sunlight filtered through the thick canopy of trees created patterns of shades in the jungle. Insects trilled and rasped, leaves whispered, little creatures walked the underbush leaving ripples of rustling and birds whistled their territorial claims. We paused for a while to check our feet and found leaches trying to grasp our feet through the holes of the lace of the shoes. Some of my friends got panic stricken but we were well guarded by the bandage off the tobacco leaves. We were forced to speed up to get rid of this insects. Shortly we reached the top of the Tandong hill at an altitude of eight thousand five hundred feet above sea level.

Amidst the dense forest on the plateau there stood a three storied high observation tower and two small monasteries an old one and the other under construction. A young lama welcomed us. Initially we thought to spend the night at the veranda of the watch tower. But later we changed our minds to honour the request of the lama and occupied the newly constructed monastery. The lama a very hospitable man offered us tea. Tandong has a unique location. Though it's only eight thousand five hundred feet high but it offers a spectacular view of the surroundings. Perhaps no other place in Sikkim offers a better panoramic view of the mountain ranges than Tandong. It's like sitting in centre of a huge amphitheatre. On the east one can see the full Chola Range, on the west the Singalila Range and the towering Kanchendzonga. In the north east can be seen the Paunhri peak with surrounding mountains. Darjeeling, Gyalshing, Nathula, a part of Gangtok and the rolling plains of Siliguri can be visible from here. Both sunrise and sunset are simply breathtaking. From other parts of Sikkim Tandong looks like a volcano and legend has it that it was once an active volcano which is now dormant. Besides all these there is another legend of the Lepcha tribe that saved itself on its summit during the great deluge that once inundated the world. The story has a resemblance with that of Noah and his Ark and Mount Arrarat which Tandong is said to be. Tandong is also worshipped by the Lepchas in a festival called "Tandong Lho Rum Faat" which literally means "Worship of Tandong".

We heard all these stories of Tandong from the Lama while we were preparing our lunch. We prepared rice. We brought tinned fish curry with us. So we had a very homely lunch after quite few days. The veranda of the Tower where we settled initially was specious enough for us. Amidst the jungle surrounded by mountain we had our lunch which we would never forget. After lunch laid down on our mattress and relaxed ay enjoyed our temporary kingdom until sunset. It was a memorable moments we could treasure in our books and volume of our memory for ever. We were mesmerized by nature. We could see the sun woke up in Bhutan and crossing over the Kanchendzonga went to Nepal for rest leaving behind several colours bands of colours. As sun set we rearranged our belongings and took shelter in the newly constructed monastery. We lit two candles inside and outside in the courtyard lit a fire for tea. With the sunset the entire jungle slipped into silence. The cacophony of birds and insects sank into silence. Besides all these there is another legend of the Lepcha tribe that saved itself on its summit during the great deluge that once inundated the world. The story has a resemblance to that of Noah and his Ark and Mount Arrarat which Tandong is said to be. Tandong is also worshipped by the Lepchas in a festival called "Tandong Lho Rum Faat" which means "Worship of Tandong".

We heard all these stories of Tandong hill from our the Lama while preparing our lunch. We prepay rice and we brought tinned fish curry with us. So we had a very homely lunch after quite a few days. The veranda of the Tower where we settled initially was specious enough for us. Amidst the forest surrounded by mountains we had our lunch that we could never forget. After lunch we laid down on our mattress and relaxed and enjoyed our temporary kingdom until sunset. It was a memorable moment that we could treasure in the books and volumes of our memory for ever. We were mesmerized by nature. We could see the sun woke up in Bhutan and crossing over the Kanchendzonga went to Nepal for rest leaving behind several bands of colours. As sun set we rearranged our belongings and took shelter in a newly constructed room of the Gompha. We lit a candle inside the room and outside in the courtyard lit a small fire for preparation of tea. With the sunset entire jungle slipped into silence. The cacophony of birds and insects also sank into silence.

Sitting indoor with tea we absorbed in chatting. Time moved on leaden feet. Darkness engulfed the entire area of the courtyard and the jungle. After a while one of friends went outside and called us. Someone asked "what's up?" He didn't reply but pointed at the sky. We looked up and saw a starry canopy above us and the milkyway spread from East to West. On the earth a heavy curtain of darkness wrapped us with everything around. Sometimes the calls of different creatures were breaking the sound silence. Altogether it's an uncanny ambience around us. All of a sudden one of us spotted the bright beam of light of his four cell tourch aiming to a sound coming from a nearby tree and drew our attention to a Himalayan flying squirrel. We all stood perplexed watching the small creature stuck to the branch of a tree. Suddenly it took a flight stretching its wings glided a few yards and vanished into the darkness. It was a unique experience to all of us. After a while we came inside the room. We had our dinner early as usual and kept all our dishes and utensils outside in the courtyard for washing next morning. We closed the door and laid down on our mattress. Night was still young and we were gossiping. Suddenly a tapping sound on the rock outside drew our attention. We became cautious and stopped talking. Yes, it's there. Outside in the courtyard a marching sound of hoofs on the rocky floor was very distinct now. What could it be? We left our bed very cautiously and leaning against the window peeped outside. To our utter surprise we discovered a herd of seven or eight spotted deer were moving around in the courtyard. They turned up here for rice gruel and rice which we left while preparing our lunch. We didn't disturb them and quietly shut the window and came back to our bed.

But two consecutive thrilling experiences kept us excited for a long time before sleep.

Next day morning we woke up early to witness the sunrise from the watch tower. Many of us have the experience to watch sunrise from the Tiger Hill in Darjeeling. In that case we have to move from Darjeeling by taxi or jeep during the dead hours of the day for Tiger Hill. But here we were at the top of the Hill. We all slowly moved through the veil of mist towards the watch tower. Darkness gradually faded out and then sky was brightening before the sun appeared on the eastern horizon of the mountain range of Bhutan. The vastness of the snow peaks before us spreading from eats to west was beyond expression. We all stood motionless as the first ray of the sun touched Mount Kanchendzonga and with its first touch it turned pink. One after another peak enlightened with the touch of sunshine and began to change colour from pink to golden and at last bright silver. We were watching the magic of nature as if we were hypnotized for the time being. When the entire range of the mountain became dazling in bright sunshine and the jungle around us woke up we came back to reality. We discended gradually from the tower and in the courtyard another surprise was waiting for us. A group of yellow beak "Chough" and "Blue Magpie" thronged around the courtyard. They were also drawn here because of rice left last night along with our utensils and plates in the courtyard. At the sound of our arrival they disappeared in the forest in a twinkle of an eye. But before they disappeared they quenched our thirst for nature. We came back to our nest and tried to prepare morning tea. After all these mesmerizing trances we had to come to our usual routine of life. Because we would leave this place now. We would go down to the world of our everyday life alienated from the soothing touch of mother nature.

*****

Lonely planet

Asis Mukherjee

"Summer kisses winter tears",and we, four, responded the summon of the mountain. We four, myself, and my friends cum colleagues, Pradip Biswas, Swapan Das alias Swapanda and Pradip's neighbour, a senior person Mr. Pal alias Palbabu, a gazetted officer always wearing a mask of gravity of his position, set out for our very familiar and famous Sandakphu and Phalut route. April didn't befull us, rather we were overwhelmed with ecstasy in the abundance of nature's gift for what trekkers around the world gather here every year. Upto Sandakphu, it was a tailor - made journey.

But the surprise was hidden for us beyond that. We reached Sandakphu on the scheduled day of our itinerary and after a shivering night the dawn appeared to unveil the face of the great " Sleeping Budda " with the magic of colours. We stood perplexed in the blowing wind to witness the magic of nature and felt as if lost in the vastness of the universe. After being rejuvenated in the warmth of the kitchen and perpetual service of tea we got our nerve back to normal.

After a heavy breakfast, we set out around eight in the morning. It was a very cool but pleasant weather all around. Today's is the longest march from Sandakphu to Phalut about twenty one kilometres. But the trail was almost flat at an altitude of 11000 feet above sea level. After a continuous march of four hours I found two young foreigners resting before the ruins of a burnt forest bungalow. When I reached, I was cordially greeted by them. I unleashed my rucksack and sat beside them. I could hardly recognize the place until they confirmed that it was Sabarkum,where once upon a time there was a forest rest house which was set to fire by the followers of Subhash Ghissing as a part of their agitation. Soon we became friends. The young man coming from Holland was a florist and the other one was a young lady of Canada came presently from Bangladesh on her way back to home. She was a student on her research work, came to Bangladesh for six months on a project to train the fishermen there about modern technique of fishing and breeding culture.

I observed that they were concentrating on a volumenous book. When asked they laid out the book towards me and told that they were planning to have a break there and they would put up in a forest bungalow near by which they found in the book and the name of the place was Molley. I was surprised at the information because before commencement of our journey I gathered latest information of the route from the office of the Tourism Department, Government of West Bengal at Dalhousie Square Kolkata. Off course I didn't find any information of either forest Bunglow or trekkers hut in their information brochure. I took the book and found in the marked page a notation of a forest bungalow and detailed information of the location which was just a furlong away from our resting place. I observed that it is a travel guide of India published by " Lonely Planet ". The Dutchman came to India with it, with an eye to roaming the land for six months. I was not only surprised, but also ashamed of my ignorance about my own land. The " lonely planet " opened another world before me which was situated very near to me but far away from my knowledge.

Instantly I made up my mind to break the journey and rest at Molley because my companions were far behind and they must be fatigued when they would come. I told them likewise and they also greeted me to rejoin them at Molley. We shook hand and they approached for Molley. After a while, when my friends appeared at my resting place with leaden feet dragging their fatigued bodies and loads on their back they got a bit surprised seeing me sitting alone in that disolate place in front of the ruined bunglow. But soon they got rejuvenated when they heard me calling it a day and we would rest at Molley forest bungalow, our new destination of the day. After a little rest we all started for Molley and in fifteen minutes walk downhill when we reached the forest rest house, I thanked Almighty for introducing me with " Lonely Planet ".

*****

A Rainy Day Out

Asis Mukherjee

It's monsoon in the Bengal and the sky was usually overcast with quick cloud. A general weather forecast was there of rain. But you can not forecast when and where and how long it will be raining. And if you remain confined to your room during those months together you will certainly get bored and can not enjoy the rainy season and can not sing or listen to either a Tagore's song on rain or a Phill Collins' famous "I wish it would rain down on me ...." Because it automatically oozes out from your heart when you are totally filled with joy.

So one dull monsoon morning we set forth for a day out. We are four consisting of myself, my wife, my son and his wife. My son Abir was on the steering. We planned to visit the house of Sarat Chandra Chattopadhyay, the stalwart writer of Bengali literature at Deulty village in our Howrah district about sixty kilometers away. We drove through the drizzle and gradually proceeded through traffic jam until we crossed the toll tax gate. After a few kilometers we got rid of the traffic jam and Abir began to drive smoothly along the national highway leading to Chennai and Mumbai. Despite the drizzle, as the wippers cleaned the windscreen, our minds were also brightened in the spirit of joy drive. We reached Deulty around 1 p.m. We parked our car and entered into the compound of the house. Though other days it's closed by twelve, but due to our good luck it was kept open for some VIP visitors. Anyway we found the enclosed garden and the two storied house was well maintained and very impressive at the first sight. We also stepped up the verandah and moved from one room to another. From the balcony of the first floor we got a nice glimpse of the river Rupnarayan. A young boy, named Tubai, the son of the caretaker, was there who was narrating us like a professional guide the stories of the great man, where he used to sit and write or meet the revolutionaries who fought for our indipendance and used to come here by that time. We took rest there for a while and then started for Kolaghat. On our way we had already seen the Damodar river and now we would see the Rupnarayan river. Within half an hour we reached Kolaghat just crossing the bridge over the river Rupnarayan. But due to continuous rain we could not stop to watch the surroundings of the Rupnarayan. We went straight to the market place in search of a good restaurant. There were many, but all were overcrowded. We could not imagine that in such bad weather so many people had come for outing. Abir contacted one of his friends and took the return lane. Within a few yards we parked our car in the parking lot and entered into a nice hotel cum restaurant. We preferred to sit in the covered garden. Indeed the place was a worth selection and whatever dishes we ordered were equally good. It's 2 p.m. at the clock now and the right time for lunch.

After having our lunch we set out on the road again bound for home. The rain had been subsided now. No hurry scurry! We drove comfortably. We paused for a while at the site of Rupnarayan and Damodar. We started again while John Denver was singing in the back ground "Country Roads Take Me Home...." Indeed we all want to go home, so a non stop drive of two hours brought us home before dusk. A day out in the rain thus remained for ever vibrant in the books and volumes of our memory.

*****

Beyond The Singalila Range

Asis Mukherjee

Where is Singalila Pass and where is Measures' Club Tent at Kolkata Maidan? But there is a link between these two places. Actually the second one is the birthplace of our plan to approach Singalila Range standing to the far north of West Bengal as a demarcating line between our state and Sikkim and Nepal also. We four were there with cup of tea at the courtyard of the club in an autumn evening. I was elaborating the idea of crossing the famous Singalila Pass to my elderly friend Pradipta Chakraborty alias Dipuda and Pradip Biswas, my friend cum colleague and partner of many treks and Pravat Ray alias Rayda, Dipuda's friend.

All of us though visited Sandakphu many times, were very much interested to my plan to cross the range and explore the unknown forest of Sikkim. Only I had once come from Versey of West Sikkim to Phalut with my friend Sunil Sen, who is no more now. So a team of four, consisting of two hexagenerian and two comparatively younger in their forties, trekkers and mountain lovers was formed and I was entrusted to book the train tickets for New Jalpaiguri according to our itinerary.

The very next day I booked our onward and return journey tickets with utter excitement. I always like to enjoy the thrill of a journey when the tickets are confirmed. On the scheduled date we all assembled at Sealdah station for Darjeeling Mail. After boarding in the train I told Dipuda, that I already informed Jeevan Chetri at Manebhanjan about our arrival. He appreciated me. Jeevan Bhai is a very popular person at Manebhanjan, who not only provides shelter and food to the trekkers but also helps them by providing information and guide or porters to them. He is a very well known person among trekkers also. Next day morning our train reached New Jalpaiguri station at right time. We came out of the station and booked a car for Manebhanjan. It's a couple of hours journey and we reached Manebhanjan about eleven. Alighting from the car we checked in Jeevan Bhai's homestay. After lunch we briefed our plan to Jeevan Bhai and asked him to arrange two porters for us. He assured us and requested us to take rest. In the afternoon we strolled along the motorable road leading to Sandakphu and noticed the check post of Singalila National Park. We came back to our nest. Meanwhile Jeevan Bhai brought two local young men to introduce us for our trek for next few days. We discussed with them about our trekking plan and they assured us to turn up next day morning. We rearranged our rucksack for the last time and went for our dinner.

Morning wore a sunny face. We woke up at Jeevan Bhai's call with steaming cups of tea. The porters also arrived for packing their loads. We got prepared to set out on the road again. After another round of tea I paid Jeevan Bhai's bill for our boarding and food and came out of the lodge. Though everybody of us trekked along this route earlier but the call of mountain made the familiar route even more interesting. We arrived at the check post and paid the entry fees and marched ahead. Dipuda and Rayda were not carrying any load. The porters were following us with their rucksacks. I along with Pradip were marching with our rucksacks on our back. We all were marching very leasurely enjoying our journey at every step. No hurry scurry, no exhaustion. In one hour and a half we reached Meghma. Aptly christened the name of the village Meghma because in Bengali it means a place in the cloud. And in fact most of the time it remains behind the curtain of a mist. We took a brief pause with a cup of tea. Our poretrs also arrived and I instructed them to march ahead towards Tumling another small village at the Indo-Nepal border avoiding the steep climb of Tonglu. We again came down on the road and soon we arrived at the bifurcation of the road where one trail to right side went to Tonglu and the left side motorable road went to Nepal. We took the left hand road and entered in to Nepal and crossing through many shops and houses, shortly we reached Tumling. It's a bright sunny place on the slope of the mountain. Here and there the demarcation stones were seen showing the names of two countries, Nepal and India. The local shopkeeper arranged our seats and the table in the courtyard of his shop and served drinks and snacks for us. We deserved it because since morning we were marching and we got fatigued also.

After a brief pause at Tumling we started again. Our next halt would be Kalipokhari and it would be today's final halt. Within three hours we comfortably reached Kalipokhari. We found numbers of hotels there and put up in one of those. The arrangements were very nice and the hospitality of the owner was also very good. These hotels were built up en route to Sandakphu with the concept of homestay in Nepal. We occupied two adjacent rooms and put our rucksacks and came to the dining place for lunch. Our porters also put up in a separate room. After lunch we came to our rooms for rest. It was our first night halt. In the evening we assembled at the lounge and ordered for tea. Everybody was very comfortable and happy. I, myself, was very much satisfied seeing Dipuda and Rayda, at their sixties performed very well in the test of the first day trek. We could not feel how a couple of hours we spent in chatting and gossiping within ourselves. Because Dipuda himself was a mine of many treasures of expeditions. We retired to bed after dinner early because we all were very tired and fatigued.

Next day morning we woke up early and received as usual our bed tea. Within an hour we got ready and set out after breakfast. Today is the last leg of ascent from 10,400 ft. to Sandakphu at 11,930 ft. the heighest point of West Bengal. But now we were accustomed to this escalation. Though today's distance is only six kilometers but the ascent was very steep. Within one hour we reached Bikebhanjan and we entered into a small hut for tea. Our senior members deserved a tea break. We took rest for some time also because our next halt would be the last halt for today. After a while we resumed our journey and gradually marched ahead. In two hours we reached our destination and checked in the trekkers' lodge and immidiately I ordered for lunch.

After lunch we relaxed on our bed. Now the ascent was over, the strains on our body was almost endured. It's enough time to relax and enjoy. Dipuda was telling his experience of his first visit to Sandakphu. It was an exhilarating experience around forty years back. We went outside as the sun was preparing to set down. With magic of colours it bade adieu to us. The cold wind from the north drove us back to our room. Evening also bought for us rounds of tea and coffee and stories from Dipuda. After having our dinner at around 8-30 we took shelter to our bed.

Next morning we were prepared to experience the sunrise from the highest point of West Bengal. In the dark of the night wrapped in woollen cover we came out from our room to welcome the sun. Cold wind was trying to drive us back to our room but we were determined to behold the sunrise. Magic of indescribable colours of the nature compelled us to stand perplexed and behold. We came back to our room for warmth and morning tea. After having our breakfast and second round of tea we set out for Phalut. It's the longest march of twenty-one kilometers of the route but almost flat above eleven thousand feet from sea level. Despite that altitude we all were moving very comfortably. All along our way we were accompanied by the beautiful Mount Kanchenjunga on our right in the clear sky of November. The cold breeze was very soothing. After a continuous march of three hours and a half we halted for a while at Sabarkhum where once a forest bungalow was there but now only the ruins remained. And there we discovered the entire panoramic view of the Himalaya expanding from Mount Kanchenjunga to Mount Everest. It was obviously a rare chance to have a glimpse of such a wide panoramic view of the Himalaya. Our mission was accomplished.

After a while we resumed our march and in two hours of continuous trek we reached Phalut trekkers hut. Immidiately I ordered for our lunch. We all were very hungry after a long march. After having our lunch we occupied our bed arranged at one side of the hall and began to revise our plan because so far though we crossed the highest point of our trek, but the route was very familiar to all of us. The real trek in that sense will start from tomorrow towards unknown. Though I came from Versey of West Sikkim crossing the Singalila Range to Phalut last year but I can't lead my team through the dense forest of Sikkim. And that's the reason of hiring two local porters cum guide who could help us to negotiate the route. In the evening we enjoyed the sunset from a different view point.

Next morning we woke up as usual and after having a heavy breakfast we set out for Singalila Range. The trek route to Gorkey took the right track down hill while ours went straight towards Toriphule at the base of Singalila Ridge. We went straight to towards Toriphule and after reaching there we paused for a while before the final ascent. We began to climb again until we reached the top of Singalila Ridge. The steep climb for an hour made us exhausted and after reaching the top of the Singalila Ridge we unleashed our rucksacks and sat down. There also we came to notice the demarcation pillar showing India's border with Nepal. The other side of the ridge extending from east to west was covered in deep forest. Dipuda asked which direction we should move now. The porters cum guides got confused and ultimately surrendered with their disability to locate the foot track through the deep forest towards Versey. Dipuda now suggested to proceed towards the west along the ridge where at the far end the "Chhiwabhanjan Pass" at the border of India and Nepal was visible from here. So we again took our rucksacks and began to march along the foot track leading towards Chhiwabhanjan. Gradually we entered into the forest as we began to discend. Keeping our direction towards west we reached Chhiwabhanjan in less than two hours. We found the Border Security Force's camp over there. Seeing two senior persons with us they cordially invited us to their mess house a farlong away beside a playground. We took shelter at their camp and got tea and biscuits very shortly. That night we spent in the room instead of the tent and fortunately had good foods also offered by our BSF Jawans.

Next morning we started our journey, after two consecutive rounds of tea and breakfast, for Utterey, a small village in the West Sikkim district. As we discended through the forest we discovered two marvels on our way, one was a forest bungalow of "Chitre" a nice place to stay amidst a small field surrounded by big trees of the forest and the other was a small rivulet coming down from Chhiwabhanjan Pass which formed "Little Rangeet" river at Jorethung. While dashing through the dense forest we realised that yesterday's discission of proceeding towards Chhiwabhanjan instead of approaching for " Khuldhap" was very much correct. Because on account of the Chhiwabhanjan Border Post this route to Utterey was apparently far better, though we were pushing through the Moss and Fern and Bush at every step. Sometimes we had to cross the rivulet on our way down. At length we came to the border of the forest where we discovered a "Trout Breading Center" of the Fisheries

Department of the Government of Sikkim. We saw the green cultivated fields of the village. It's almost a flat stretch of land extended up to the houses of the village. We gradually discended and came through it. Soon we discovered the "Green Valley Resort" a nice hotel located at a quiet and nice place. We checked in with leaden feet and we all again thanked Dipuda for his correct discission at the right time. Now it's our time to celebrate and recapitulate the essence of our hard trek through the unknown. Because tomorrow we will leave this heavenly place and return to our usual place of din and bustle.

*****

Trek to tholung

Asis Mukherjee

When our north Sikkim bound bus dropped us at Mangan, the District Head Quarter of North Sikkim, we found the place as desolate as a remote village on the hill. We found neither a hotel nor a lodge but only a few shops by the roadside. We entered one tea shop and on enquiry we came to know that we had to put up at the nearby school building. So we went to the headmaster's quarter to approach him for our night stay. The headmaster was a very gentleman and when we explained our purpose to come here, he gladly opened a room for us. We put up our rucksacks and set out again for the District Magistrate's Office to obtain our permission to go to the Dzongu valley which is a restricted area for the Lepchas and any outsider must have to take permission from the local government authority. We explained to him our objective to visit the Tholung Monastery and applied in writing and got the permission easily. We again came to the tea shop and asked for a cup of tea. With the cup of tea we sat together and were discussing our future plans. Until that time we did not know where we would put up the next day.

In the year 1997 this place was not known to even trekkers and mountain lovers though tour operators were taking the tourists from Gangtok to Gurudongmar lake and Yumthang valley in the North Sikkim. Even today though communication systems have developed and internet service is available to everybody, Tholung Monastery remains in the age of the hoary past. The monastery was built in the early part of the eighteenth century in the reign of Chogyal Chakdor Namgyal. I got this information in the guide book of Sikkim written by Rajesh Verma. The mystery of the monastery drew my attention to visit the remote place in North Sikkim district. So myself along with my friend Pradip Biswas set out one day for Gangtok during autumn. After taking one day's rest at Gangtok we came here. Now we are sitting at the tea shop and talking within ourselves about tomorrow's plan. A gentleman was sitting beside us with his cup of tea. Hearing our discussion in bengali he interrupted also in bengali and asked us where we were going to. We were very much surprised to find a Bengalee at that place which was quite beyond our expectations. He then introduced himself as an officer of the Central Intelligence Branch, Government of India. He was posted at Mangan on duty. Hearing our intention to visit Tholung Monastery he generously came forward to our rescue. He took us with him to the house of the local M. L. A. Before leaving he told the shopkeeper for three meals for all of us for the night. We understood that he used to eat there. So we also got relieved from the tension of our dinner. We followed him and within a furlong on the main road we entered into a big two storey building. A man opened the door and took us inside the house and told us to wait in the drawing room. After a while a gentleman appeared and greeted us. After hearing our purpose he called a man and introduced us with him and told us that he would take us next morning to Lingzey village where his brother was staying. Not only that he also assured us that his brother would help us in every need and we were supposed to stay at his brother's house. After having a cup of tea offered to us we thanked him and left his house. We thanked the I . B. Officer and came along with him to the tea shop again. After having our dinner together we came to our night stay at the school. I told my friend Pradip that there is a local belief that "you can go to Tholung only when Tholung calls you". Before going to bed we thanked God for making such an arrangement for us which was beyond our imagination. Now we can also feel the call of Tholung in our hearts.

Next day morning we woke up and got prepared to set out. Before leaving we bade goodbye to the Headmaster and conveyed our thanks. We came to the house of the M. L. A. and found the man who was entrusted to accompany us was waiting for our arrival. We all moved a few yards down the road and waited for the service jeep for Lingzey. The jeep came from Gangtok. A few passengers alighted and we got in. Within an hour we reached our destination, the Lingzey village. Our guide took us to the house of the brother of the M. L. A. It was also a big two storied building. We entered and the guide introduced us to him and he cordially welcomed us to his house. In no time we were served with tea in a nice mug. The landlord accompanied us and asked me why we were going to visit the Tholung monastery. Because the local people of the state, especially the Lepchas used to go there. It's a very sacred pilgrimage to them. I told him that I read about it in a guide book of Sikkim written by Rajesh Verma and Tholung monastery attracted me since then. He appreciated our intention but he also informed us that this year the "Kamsil " festival was over in the month of April. "Kamsil " festival takes place every three year when the relics and the artifacts are displayed for the pilgrims. I told him that I was aware of that. I also added that the mystery of the monastery drew me here. He assured us that the next day we would move for Tholung and the man who brought us here would accompany us as our guide. It's a day long march of twenty kilometers.

We went to our room provided by our host on the first floor. Putting down our rucksacks at one corner we relaxed on our mattress. In fact we could not perceive how smoothly everything was happening so far on our way beyond our expectations. After lunch was served in our room we set out for a stroll around. At first we went to a little monastery adjacent to the house where a group of young boys, dressed in saffron garments were studying. It appeared to us like a hostel cum school where training and schooling both were provided to the future lamas. It was run by our host. Then we strolled around the Lepcha village in the Dzongu valley. We also saw the famous Lingzey waterfall which was pouring its water into the torrential Tholung river. We came across the "Beh Forest Bungalow". After a brief stroll we came back to our nest before dusk. In the evening we were served with typical Lepcha dishes and drinks. In Lepcha the name of the drink was "Chee". It's a kind of local beer served in a bamboo container with a straw to sip. Along with it there were "Thukpa " and "Momo" which were rather known to us. With that we finished our dinner and went to bed.

Next morning after a heavy breakfast we set out for our final destination accompanied by our guide. We crossed the Tholung river on a bamboo bridge.The path went through the forest and cardamom groves. Here and there the rocky cliffs were to be negotiated with great caution. Sometimes waterfalls were descending down below to the Tholung river which was our company all through the way. Birds tweeted loudly in the bush and on the branches of the trees. Here and there we found huts of the hardy lepcha families. We paused for a while at one of them for tea. Since we left Mangan we did not spend a single penny to anyone. We had been treated as guests of the entire region. We reached Tholung monastery on the top of the hill at around 2 p.m. The newly built Monastery stood with an adjacent bungalow for the pilgrims on a flat land surrounded by prayer flags and a small tomb stood at another side. We unleashed our rucksacks and sat at the doorstep of the monastery. Its height is 8000 feet. In the clear sky towering Kanchenjunga and Siniolchu peaks were seen clearly from here. All around only silence prevailed. This place is more a pilgrimage than a tourist spot. A young Buddhist Monk came out from the monastery and our guide introduced us to him. He cordially invited us inside the house. Shortly he offered us noodles and tea. We all were fatigued and hungry also. So we devoured the meal silently. After that food we regained some energy. We went inside the Holy Monastery and there we met a senior Lama. We saw the metal "Chorten" in which enclosed the ashes of Lama Latsun Chembo the patron saint of Sikkim and thirteen boxes containing the holy relics and artifacts under supervision of the Government of Sikkim. Every three year these artifacts are unveiled to the public during the "Kamsil" Ceremony in the month of April. The "Thangkas"were hanging all around. The environment inside the monastery was very quiet and peaceful and a fragrance of incense was prevailing all around. After spending some time we came out side to enjoy the beauty of the nature. We realised why the Sikkimes had chosen this place to keep the relics and the artifacts protected from the invading Nepalese. It was so secluded and perhaps due to high altitude and dense forest it was easy to guard. The calmness of the nature soothes one's heart. Our guide told us that a few miles walk further from here along the Tholung river takes one to a religious spot called "Devta Pani". But we were satisfied that we could reach Tholung through many odds and uncertainty. So we were sitting there until sunset. When darkness engulfed the entire area and a starry canopy was spread in the sky we went to our night shelter. Our guide lit a fire and we all sat around it with a cup of tea. It was like celebration of a bonfire. Our guide and the young lama started to prepare food for our dinner. They didn't allow us to participate. So we sat and watched them. Around 8 p.m. we had our supper and then we went to bed and slept in the lap of the Lama Latsun Chembo. Dawn appeared quietly in the silent valley. We came out from the room. Our guide offered us the morning tea. We enjoyed the morning sunshine on the Mount Kanchenjunga. After breakfast we bade good bye to the monks of the monastery and started our return journey to Lingzey. We reached Lingzey at around 2 p.m. We came to the house of our host. He requested us to stay for the night also. But as we saw the jeep was available for Gangtok we decided to leave. We expressed our thanks and bade adieu to him. As our jeep started for Gangtok our sojourn through a trance to the land of mystery came to the end leaving a permanent image in our minds.

*****

গোঁসাইকুন্ডের পথে

আশিস মুখার্জী

২৩শে সেপ্টেম্বর দ্রুতলয়ে অফিস থেকে ফিরেই যখন পিঠে রুকস্যাক নিয়ে বেরিয়ে পড়লাম তখন অঝোর ধারায় বৃষ্টি পড়ছে। এবারের গন্তব্য নেপালের গোঁসাই কুন্ড। ট্রেন নির্ধারিত সময়েই ছাড়লো। পরদিন সকাল দশটা নাগাদ পৌঁছাল রক্সৌল। এখন মিথিলা এক্সপ্রেস রক্সৌল পর্যন্ত আসছে। আগে গাড়ি বদল করতে হতো। স্টেশন থেকে বেরিয়ে রিক্সায় কাস্টমসের বেড়া ডিঙিয়ে ওপারে বীরগঞ্জ। তখনই বুঝলাম ফেরার সময় কপালে দুর্ভোগ আছে। কেননা আমার সঙ্গে বিদেশি ক্যামেরা আছে। অনেক অনুনয়েও কোনো লিখিত অনুমতি পত্র পাওয়া গেল না। অর্থাৎ ফিরতি পথে প্রণামী দিতেই হবে। সে যা হওয়ার হবে। আরও অনেকেই তো যাচ্ছে। পথিমধ্যে দালাল এসে বাসের টিকিট ধরিয়ে দিয়ে গেল। বীরগঞ্জ কাঠমান্ডু নাইট সার্ভিস। বিশাল তোরণ পেরিয়ে নেপালে প্রবেশ করে বাস টার্মিনাসের কাছেই যাত্রার বিরতি। রিক্সা থেকে নামতেই দুই বন্ধু জুটলো। যোগাযোগের সুত্রও পরিচয় হতেই বেরিয়ে এলো। এরা দুজন যাবে এভারেস্ট বেসক্যাম্প ও গোকিও লেক। আপাতত একই সঙ্গে কাঠমান্ডু। একজনের জিম্মায় মালপত্র রেখে দুজনে গেলাম টাকা পরিবর্তনের জন্য ব্যাঙ্কে। যদিও নেপালের অনেক জায়গাতেই ভারতীয় টাকা চলে তবুও বদল করে রাখা ভালো। তারপর খাওয়ার পালা সাঙ্গ করে পথের ধারে কলে একে একে স্নান সেরে নিয়ে অপেক্ষা কখন বাসের সময় হয়। দুই বন্ধুর একজন অপেক্ষাকৃত অভিজ্ঞ পাহাড়ের পথে। গতবছর সেই এসেছিল ল্যাংট্যাং উপত্যকায়। তারই দেওয়া ম্যাপ হাত ঘুরে এখন আমার পকেটে। গোঁসাই কুন্ড যাবার পরিকল্পনা এবং উৎসাহ আমার অগ্রজ প্রবীণ হিমালয় পথিক শ্রীযুক্ত প্রদীপ্ত চক্রবর্তীর দেওয়া। নাইট সার্ভিসের বাস নির্ধারিত সময়ের ঘন্টা দেড়েক পরে প্রায় সাড়ে ছটায় ছাড়লো বীরগঞ্জ। পরদিন অর্থাৎ ২৫শে সেপ্টেম্বর বেলা সাড়ে আটটা নাগাদ বাস এসে কাঠমান্ডুর নতুন বাসস্ট্যান্ডে আমাদের নামিয়ে দিল। ইতিমধ্যে নেপালের সময়ের সঙ্গে ঘড়ি মিলিয়ে পনের মিনিট সময় এগিয়ে নিয়েছি। বাসষ্ট্যান্ডের বিপরীতেই অগুণতি হোটেল। টেলিফোনের বুথ দেখেই বাড়িতে কথা বলার লোভ সামলাতে পারলাম না। ফেরার সম্ভাব্য তারিখ ৬ই অক্টোবর জানিয়ে দিলাম। কেননা রক্সৌল নেমেই আমি ফেরার টিকিট করে রেখেছিলাম। দেড়শো টাকায় একটা হোটেলের ঘর দখল করে স্নান সেরেই আবার পথে। কালকের বাসের টিকিট কাটতে হবে। আমার গন্তব্য সিয়াব্রুবেনসি আর

বন্ধুরা যাবে জিরি। আমার টিকিট সামনের বালাজু বাসস্ট্যান্ড থেকে সহজেই পেয়ে গেলাম। কিন্তু বন্ধুদের টিকিটের জন্য যেতে হলো পুরনো বাসস্ট্যান্ডে। লুকলা থেকে ফেরার টিকিট হলো প্রাইভেট এয়ারলাইন্সে। নেপালে প্রায় সাত আটটা প্রাইভেট এয়ারলাইন্স আছে যারা আভ্যন্তরীণ বিভিন্ন রুটে তাদের সার্ভিস চালায় এবং সবকটাতেই বেশ ভীড়। সারাটাদিন এইভাবেই কেটে গেল। সন্ধ্যাবেলা আর এক দফা জিনিসপত্র গুছিয়ে নেওয়া হলো। অতিরিক্ত কিছু জিনিস হোটেলের জিম্মায় রেখে দিলাম। ফেরার সময় নিয়ে নেওয়া যাবে। তাড়াতাড়ি রাতের খাওয়া সাঙ্গ করে যে যার বিছানা নিলাম কেননা পরদিন ভোরেই যাত্রা শুরু।

ট্যাক্সি বলা ছিল। পরদিন ভোরবেলা অন্ধকার থাকতেই ড্রাইভার এসে হাজির। পথের বন্ধুদের হাত মিলিয়ে শুভেচ্ছা জানিয়ে বিদায় দিলাম। আমার বেরোতে এখনো ঘণ্টা খানেক দেরি আছে। বিছানায় গা এলিয়ে আকাশ পাতাল ভাবতে ভাবতে চোখ বুজে এসেছিল। হাতের ঘড়িতে এলার্ম বাজতেই চটকা ভেঙে গেল। রুকস্যাক গোছানোই ছিল। বাইরে বেরিয়ে এক কাপ চা খেয়ে সোজা বাসষ্ট্যান্ডে। নির্ধারিত বাস, নির্দিষ্ট সিট। অতএব বাসের ছাদে স্যাক তুলে দিয়ে ভেতরে গিয়ে বসি। একেবারে পিছনে সিট পড়েছে। কি আর করা যাবে! স্থানীয় লোকজন ছাড়া জনা ছয়েক ট্রেকার রয়েছে বাসে। সবাই বিদেশি। কেবল মাত্র আমেরিকা থেকে একটি অল্প বয়সী মেয়ে একা এসেছে। সঙ্গে একজন নেপালী যুবক গাইড। আর আমিও চলেছি একা। তবে এদের সবারই গন্তব্য ল্যাংট্যাং উপত্যকা । আমি এখনও জানিনা ল্যাংট্যাং ও গোঁসাইকুন্ড দু' জায়গাতেই একবারে যেতে পারবো কিনা। যদিও প্রদীপ্তদা সেইভাবেই আমার ট্রেক সূচী কোলকাতায় করে দিয়েছিলেন। কিন্তু কোলকাতায় বসে একরকম পরিকল্পনা করা যায় আর পথে নেমে তা অনেক সময়ই ওলটপালট হয়ে যায়। যেমন আমার একটা দিন কালই খরচ হয়ে গেছে কাঠমান্‌ডুতে। আজ ২৬শে সেপ্টম্বর। বাস সাড়ে ছ'টাতেই ছাড়লো। সারা দিন বাস মন্থর গতিতে চলল। বিরক্তিকর এই রকম বাস যাত্রা। বিকেল নাগাদ রামচে চেকপোস্ট। এবার আমরা ল্যাংট্যাং সংরক্ষিত এলাকায় প্রবেশ করবো। আমি ছাড়া আর সব বিদেশি যাত্রীকেই মাথা পিছু নেপালী মুদ্রায় ছ'শো পঞ্চাশ টাকা প্রবেশ কর দিতে হলো। বন্ধু রাষ্ট্রের নাগরিক বলে আমার ছাড়। প্রায় সন্ধ্যা নাগাদ বাস ধুনচের বেশ কিছুটা আগে থেমে গেল। সামনে ধ্বস আছে। বাস আর যাবে না। পায়ে হেটে ধ্বস পেরিয়ে আবার বাকি পথ অন্য বাস নিয়ে যাবে। অগত্যা পথে নামা। নেমে দেখি আরো বাসের যাত্রীরা ধ্বস পেরিয়ে ওপারে যাচ্ছে। তার মধ্যে অন্য বাসে আসা অনেক বিদেশী ট্রেকারও রয়েছে। ধ্বস পেরিয়ে বাসে উঠলাম। সন্ধ্যার অন্ধকার নেমে এসেছে। ধুনচে আরো আধ ঘন্টার রাস্তা। আর সিয়াব্রুবেনসি আরো দেড়

ঘণ্টা। যদিও ল্যাংট্যাং যেতে হলে সিয়াব্রুবেনসি যাওয়াই ভালো কিন্তু কেন জানিনা ল্যাংট্যাংএর সব পদবযাত্রীরা ধুনচেতেই নামলো। অর্থাৎ এখানে থেকেই তারা ট্রেকিং শুরু করবে। আমিও সাতপাঁচ ভেবে বাস থেকে নেমে পড়লাম। রাত সাড়ে সাতটা। অর্থাৎ তেরো ঘণ্টা লাগলো এই পথটুকু আসতে। পকেটে হোটেল 'ল্যাংট্যাং ভিউ" এর কার্ড ছিল। তাই অন্ধকারের মধ্যে জিগ্যেস করে সোজা ওখানে। এক ঝাঁক ট্যুরিস্ট নামলো দেখলাম, তারা সব কোথায় অন্ধকারে সেঁধিয়ে গেলো কে জানে। হোটেলের ম্যানেজার কাম মালিক বদ্রী ঘিমেরের সঙ্গে দেখা হয়ে গেল কাউন্টারেই। আমি কার্ডটা দেখিয়ে বললাম ঘরের কথা। "কিন্তু ঘরতো নেই।" "তবে?" বললেন," দাঁড়ান, আপনি যখন একা আছেন তখন দেখি যদি অন্য কারো ঘরে ঢুকিয়ে দেওয়া যায়।" আমার আপত্তি আছে কিনা জেনেনিলেন। আমার আবার আপত্তি! তখন একটা বিছানা পেলেই হয়! এক ফরাসী ভদ্রলোক খাচ্ছিলেন আরো জানা চারেকের সঙ্গে একটা টেবিলে। তাকে গিয়ে বদ্রী আমার কথা জানিয়ে বললেন, " আমার এক বন্ধু এসে পড়েছেন। যদি আপনি আপনার ঘরে ওকেও একটু ঠাঁই দেন।" দেখলাম ফরাসী ভদ্রলোক রাজী হলেন। খুবই সজ্জন বলতে হবে! খাওয়া ছেড়ে উঠে গিয়ে আমায় ঘরের চাবি খুলে দিলেন। দেখলাম বেশ বড়ো ঘর। ঘরে চারটে শয্যা। একটি ওনার দখলে আর বাকি গুলো ফাঁকা। অর্থাৎ আমার মতো উনিও একাই পথিক। আমিও বিনা বাক্যব্যয়ে একটি শয্যার দখল নিয়ে নীচে এলাম। বিরাট ডাইনিং হল। দুটো হ্যাজাক জ্বলছে। আর টেবিলে টেবিলে জ্বলছে মোমবাতি। প্রায় সব টেবিলই দখলে। চারিদিকে চোখ বুলিয়ে দেখলাম। মনে হলো যেন কোন ইউরোপীয়ান ট্রেকার্স মিট হচ্ছে। মাঝে মধ্যে দুএকজন নেপালী যুবক। তারা হয় পোর্টার না হয় গাইড। এক কোনায় গিয়ে বসলাম এক কাপ চা নিয়ে। আমার পাশে বসে আছেন দুই ভদ্রমহিলা। বেলজিয়াম থেকে এসেছেন। দু'জনেই শিক্ষিকা। সঙ্গে তিনটি নেপালী যুবক। সবাই বিয়ার নিয়ে আড্ডায় মশগুল। এনারা ল্যাংট্যাং ঘুরে এসেছেন। তিব্বতি রুটি আর ওমলেট দিয়ে রাতের খাওয়া শেষ করে ঐ ভীড় থেকে বেরিয়ে এলাম বাইরের বারান্দায়। সেখানে কাউন্টারে বসে বদ্রীর ছেলে আর মেয়ে। তারা নিজেদের মধ্যে কি কথা বলছে আর হেসে গড়িয়ে পড়ছে। দ্বিতীয় দফার চা শেষ করে আমি সোজা নিজের ঘরে গিয়ে বিছানায়। আমার রুমমেট আমার আগেই চলে এসেছেন। উনিও ল্যাংট্যাং থেকে ঘুরে এসেছেন। চোখ বন্ধ করলাম কেননা কাল থেকে নামতে হবে পথে।

পরদিন যথারীতি ভোরে উঠে প্রাতঃকৃত্যাদি সেরে একেবারে স্যাক গুছিয়ে নীচে নেমে এলাম। চা জলখাবারের অর্ডার দিয়ে মনের ভাবনাগুলো আর একবার গুছিয়ে নিলাম। কেননা কাল রাতেই ঠিক করেছি যে মাত্র সাতদিন

সময় নিয়ে ল্যাংট্যাং গোঁসাইকুন্ড দুটো জায়গা আমার পক্ষে করা সম্ভব হবে না। আবার গোঁসাই কুন্ড গেলেও দিন বেশী হয়ে যাবে। কেননা আমায় ৩রা অক্টোবর ফিরতে হবে কাঠমান্ডুতে। আবার এদিকে শুনলাম ২ ও ৩ অক্টোবর বাস বন্ধ থাকবে দশেরা উপলক্ষে। তাই একটা উপায় আমি কাল রাতেই ভেবে রেখেছি। তা' হলো এই পথে আর না ফেরা। তাহলে আমার বাড়তি দিনগুলো কাঠমান্ডুতে বসে থাকতেও হয় না আবার সেই বিরক্তিকর বারো চোদ্দো ঘণ্টার বাস জার্নির ধকলও পোয়াতে হয় না। আমি গোঁসাই কুন্ডের ওপরে যে পাস আছে তা' পেরিয়ে হাটা পথেই পৌঁছে যাবো সুন্দরীজল। আর সেখান থেকে কাঠমান্ডু মাত্র ঘণ্টা দুয়েকের বাস রাস্তা। এখন বদ্রীর সঙ্গে একটু আলোচনা করে নিতে হবে। আর ওর কাছ থেকে পথের হদিসও জেনে নিতে হবে। ব্রেকফাস্ট খেতে খেতে বদ্রীর সঙ্গে আলোচনা সেরে নিলাম। বদ্রীও আমার সিদ্ধান্তই সমর্থন করলো। উপরন্ত আমার হাতে একটা সুন্দর ম্যাপ তুলে দিয়ে আমার যাত্রা পথের বিরতিগুলো বুঝিয়ে দিল। আমার পরিবর্তিত যাত্রাপথে ৬ দিন সময় লাগবে। অর্থাৎ আমার হাতে একটা পুরো দিন নিজের ইচ্ছে মত কাটাবার সময় রইল। হোটেলের বারান্দা থেকে ল্যাংট্যাং ও লিরুং এবং গনেশ হিমাল সুন্দর দেখা যাচ্ছে। দ্রুত কয়েকটা ছবি তুলে নিয়ে হোটেলের বিল মিটিয়ে পথে নেমে এলাম। খানিকটা গিয়েই ল্যাংট্যাং এর দিকের রাস্তা ছেড়ে নির্দেশমতো ডানহাতি পায়ে চলা পথ ধরলাম। আজকের গন্তব্য সিংগোম্ফা। বদ্রীর রুটম্যাপের নির্দেশ মতো পাঁচ ঘন্টার পথ। এখন বাজে সাড়ে আটটা। অর্থাৎ প্রায় প্রায় দুটো বাজবে সিংগোম্ফা পৌঁছাতে। একটু দেরি হলো প্রথম দিন পথে নামতে। ধুনচের মূল রাস্তা ছাড়তেই রাস্তায় আর লোকজন নেই। হাল্কা জঙ্গল শুরু হলো। তার মধ্যে দিয়ে পথ। রাস্তা ভালো। জঙ্গলের মধ্যে দিয়ে চলতে ভালোই লাগছে। অদ্‌ভুত নির্জনতা; চারিদিকে এক অদ্‌ভুত নৈঃশব্দ্য বিরাজ করছে। মাঝে মাঝে জঙ্গল ঘন হচ্ছে। দু' ঘণ্টা চলার পর পেলাম একটা চায়ের দোকান। জায়গার নাম দেওরালি। ক্ষণিকের বিরতি। আরো এক ঘন্টা চলার পর দিমসা। এখানে একটু জিরিয়ে নিয়ে আর আধ ঘন্টার একটা চড়াই ভেঙে পৌছালাম সিংগোম্ফা। ছোট্ট গ্রাম। তারই মধ্যে একাধিক বেশ সুন্দর হোটেল। ঘর নিয়ে, জিনিসপত্র রেখে গৃহকর্তার বাড়িতে এলাম দুপুরের খাওয়ার জন্য। হোটেলে কয়েকজন বিদেশি ট্রেকারকেও দেখলাম। বিকেলের দিকে দেখি দু'জন ভদ্রলোক ও একজন ভদ্রমহিলা এলেন নীচের দিক থেকে। এনাদেরকে আমি সকালে ধুনচের হোটেলে দেখেছিলাম। এনারা এসেছেন আমেরিকা থেকে। আমি ভেবেছিলাম সব বিদেশিদের মতো এনারাও ল্যাংট্যাং যাচ্ছেন। এখন দেখছি এরাও আমার পথেরই পথিক। তবে যে কোন কারণেই হোক এই ত্রয়ী কে আমার ঠিক পছন্দ হলো না। তাই কোন

আলাপচারিতায় না গিয়ে আমি আমার মতো ঘুরে বেড়াতে লাগলাম। আমি যেখানে উঠেছি সেখানে দুই যুবকের সঙ্গে আলাপ হলো। একজন এসেছে ইংল্যান্ড থেকে আর একজন এসেছে ক্যানাডা থেকে। এরা ল্যাংট্যাং ঘুরে এখানে এসেছে গোঁসাই কুন্ড যাবার উদ্দেশ্যে। সন্ধ্যা নামতেই বেশ ঠাণ্ডা অনুভব হলো। ধুনচের উচ্চতা ১৯৫০ মিটার আর সিংগোল্ফা ৩৩৫০ মিটার। অর্থাৎ আজই ১৪০০ মিটার উঠে এসেছি। তাড়াতাড়ি রাতের খাওয়া সাঙ্গ করে নিজের ঘরে গিয়ে ঢুকলাম। রাতে ভালো ঘুম হলো না। দীর্ঘ রাত অবশ্য একসময় শেষ হলো। একেবারে তৈরি হয়ে বাইরে এলাম। চা খেয়ে হোটেলের পয়সা মিটিয়ে বেড়িয়ে পড়লাম। একটু ওপর থেকে শেষ বারের মতো দেখে নিলাম সিংগোম্ফাকে। এখানে একটা চীজ উৎপাদন কেন্দ্র আছে। অনেককেই কিনতে দেখলাম। ছবি তুলে পথের দিকে নজর দিলাম। এখানে থেকে গোঁসাই কুন্ড পাঁচ সাড়ে পাঁচ ঘণ্টার পথ। তিন ঘণ্টার মাথায় ছোলাংপট্টি। চায়ের দোকান আছে দুটো। প্রয়োজনে থাকাও যায়। সকালের ঠান্ডা হাওয়ায় আর দ্রুত পদচারণায় ঘণ্টা দেড়েকের মধ্যে এসে গেলাম ছোলাংপট্টি। এখানেই আমার ব্রেকফাস্টের সাময়িক বিরতি। এখানে পৌঁছানোর একটু আগেই একটা রাস্তা উত্তর দিক থেকে এসে এই পথে মিশেছে দেখেছি। ম্যাপে মিলিয়ে দেখলাম সেটা এসেছে সিয়াব্রু থেকে। সিয়াব্রু হলো ল্যাংট্যাং পথের প্রথম যাত্রাবিরতি। অর্থাৎ যারা ল্যাংট্যাং থেকে গোঁসাই কুন্ড আসবে তারা আবার ধুনচে না ফিরে সরাসরি এ পথে চলে আসবে। চা খেয়ে, ছবি তুলে আবার যাত্রা শুরু। কাল থেকে এখনও পর্যন্ত কোন বরফাবৃত পাহাড়ের দেখা পাইনি। কেবল জঙ্গলের পথেই হেটেছি। আরো প্রায় ঘন্টা খানেক হাঁটার পর দেখলাম বড়ো গাছের রাজত্ব শেষ। অর্থাৎ দশ হাজার ফুটের ওপরে উঠে এসেছি। এদিকে আবহাওয়াও খুব খারাপ হয়ে এলো। আকাশ আর মাটি ঘন মেঘের আবরণে ঢেকে গেল। দ্রুত পা চালাতেই দেখি সামনে হোটেল "মাউন্টেন ভিউ'। ব্যবস্থা খুব ভালো নয়। কিন্তু আশ্রয়টার খুব প্রয়োজন ছিল। ঘরে ঢুকে আগে খাবারের অর্ডার দিলাম। আর শুরু হলো বৃষ্টি। আমি সঙ্গে সঙ্গেই ঠিক করে নিলাম আজ এই পর্যন্তই থাক। যদিও এখান থেকে গোঁসাই কুন্ড আর মাত্রই ঘণ্টা দুয়েকের পথ এবং আমি ভেবেওছিলাম যে গোঁসাই কুন্ডে দুদিন থাকবো। অতএব দিনের বাকি সময়টুকু আগুনের পাশে শুয়েই কাটিয়ে দিলাম রেডিও শুনে। বৃষ্টির বেগ কখনো বাড়ছে, কখনো কমছে। একসময় সন্ধ্যা নামলো। আর এখানকার রীতি অনুযায়ী সন্ধা নামতেই রাতের খাওয়া সেরে আর এক প্রস্থ চা খেয়ে আমিও শয্যা নিলাম। পরদিন ভোরে উঠে বাইরে বেরোতেই বিস্ময়ে স্তব্ধ। কাল রাতে একবারও মনে হয়নি এতো সুন্দর একটা সকাল আমার জন্য অপেক্ষা করে আছে। লৌরিবিনায়ক জায়গাটা একটা গিরিশিরার ওপরে।

উত্তর পশ্চিম দিক থেকে উত্তর পূর্ব কোণ পর্যন্ত অনর্গল দৃষ্টি চলে যায়। আর সেই দুষ্টিপথে একে একে ভেসে ওঠে অন্নপূর্ণা, মছ্‌পুছারে, গণেশ হিমাল, তিব্বতের পর্বত প্রাচীর, ল্যাংট্যাং ২ ল্যাংট্যাং ১ ও লিরুং। কাল লৌরিবিনায়কে থাকার সিদ্ধান্ত সার্থক। তাড়াতাড়ি ক্যামেরা বার করে কয়েকটা ছবি তুলে নিলাম। আজ মাত্র ঘণ্টা দুয়েকের পথ। তবু সকাল সকাল চা খেয়ে পয়সা মিটিয়ে দিয়ে পথে নেমে পড়লাম। পথ সোজা উঠে গেছে গিরিশিরার মাথায়। ধীরে ধীরে সেখানে উঠে এলাম। একটা ছোট গুম্ফা রয়েছে এখানে। তার দরজা বন্ধ। নীচে থেকে ওঠবার সময়েই ওপরে দুজনকে দেখে ছিলাম। কাছে এসে পরিচয় হলো। এক ভদ্রলোক সস্ত্রীক এসেছেন আমেরিকা থেকে। ওনারা সুন্দরীজল থেকে যাত্রা শুরু করে গোঁসাই কুন্ড হয়ে নীচে নামছেন। অর্থাৎ আমারই পথ তবে যাত্রা উল্টো দিক থেকে। এই পথে এই প্রথম গোঁসাই কুন্ডের যাত্রীর দেখা পেলাম। এখন পাহাড়ের দৃশ্য আরো পরিষ্কার, আরো উদ্ভাসিত। আর এক প্রস্থ ছবি তোলার পর যে যার গন্তব্যের দিকে অগ্রসর হলাম। এরপর আর বিশেষ চড়াই উৎরাই নেই। গত দুদিনে কোথাও এতটুকু উৎরাই পাইনি। এখন তাই সকালের নরম রোদে হাঁটতে বেশ ভালো লাগছে। খানিকটা পথ যাবার পর দেখলাম ডানদিকের পাহাড়শ্রেণী দুরে সরে গিয়ে এক গিরিখাতের সৃষ্টি করেছে। অদুরে একটা ঝর্ণা দেখা যাচ্ছে। একটা ছোট্ট সরোবর থেকে জলধারা নেমে এসে গিরিখাতের মধ্যে দিয়ে পথ করে নিয়েছে। এতক্ষণ এরই শব্দ শোনা যাচ্ছিল। এখন সমগ্র দৃশ্য বেশ স্পষ্ট হয়ে উঠেছে। আর একটু এগোতেই দেখি পথের ডান দিকে এক মাঝারি আকারের নীল, গভীর জলাশয়। বিপরীত দিকের পাহাড় সরাসরি সরোবরের গর্ভে নেমে এসেছে। চারিদিকে ইতঃস্তত পাথর পতনের চিহ্ন। এখান থেকেই অতিরিক্ত জলরাশি নীচের ছোট্ট সরোবরে জলের যোগান দিচ্ছে চারিদিক নিস্তব্ধ, জনবসতির চিহ্ন নেই কেন? এটাই কি গোঁসাই কুন্ড? কিন্তু তাহলে লোকবসতির চিহ্ন নেই কেন? সন্দিগ্ধ মনে পা চালাই। পথ ভুল হলো না তো? কিন্তু আর কোনো পথরেখাও তো নেই। অচিরেই ভুল ভাঙ্গলো। আধ ফার্লং পথ পা চালিয়ে একটু উঁচু জায়গাতে উঠে আসতেই চোখের সামনে দিগন্ত প্রসারিত হয়ে গেল। আর সেই প্রশস্ত দিগন্ত জুড়ে বিস্তৃত বিশাল এক নীল সরোবর সূর্যের আলোয় প্রতিফলিত। প্রথম দর্শনেই দারুন ভালো লেগে গেল গোঁসাই কুন্ডকে। পা চালিয়ে নেমে এলাম হোটেল "লেক সাইড"'এ। আরো কয়েকটা হোটেল আছে এখানে। তবে অবস্থানের বিচারে এটাই শ্রেষ্ঠ কাঠের বাড়ি, টিনের চাল। একটা ঘরে স্যাক রেখে খাবারের অর্ডার দিয়ে বাইরে বেঞ্চে এসে বসলাম। আকাশের অবস্থা ভালো নয়। সূর্য মাঝে মধ্যেই মেঘের আড়ালে মুখ লুকোচ্ছে। আর তখনই ঠান্ডা অনুভূত হচ্ছে। এখানকার উচ্চতা ৪৩৮০ মিটার। ঠিক গোঁসাই কুন্ডের পাড়ে বসে হিমালয়ের তুষারাবৃত

চুড়াগুলো নজরে আসে না। কেননা চারিদিকে উঁচু পাথরের পাঁচিলে ঘেরা। আমি এসেছি পশ্চিম দিক থেকে; যাবো পূর্ব দক্ষিণ কোণ দিয়ে যে রাস্তাটা দৃষ্টির আড়ালে চলে গেছে এ পথে। ঐ পথেই পড়বে আমার সর্বোচ্চ বিন্দু ৪৬০৯ মিটার। আর পড়বে সূর্য কুন্ড। সে সব আগামী কালের কথা। আজ এখন এই পূণ্য হ্রদের চারপাশ সুন্দর পাথর সাজানো পথে পরিক্রমা করে আসি। পূরাণে কথিত আছে যে যখন শিব সতীর দেহ নিয়ে উন্মত্তের মতো ঘুরে বেড়াচ্ছেন তখন একবার অত্যন্ত তৃষ্ণার্ত বোধ করায় আপন ত্রিশূলের আঘাতে সৃষ্টি করেন এই সরোবর। তাই হিন্দুদের কাছে এ অতি পূণ্য তীর্থ। যদিও একটিমাত্র শিবলিঙ্গ আছে, আর আছে একটি গুম্ফা। এই অঞ্চলের অনেক বসতিই তিব্বতি শরণার্থীদের দখলে । ফলে এই অঞ্চলে তিব্বতি বৌদ্ধদের আধিপত্য বেশি। পরিক্রমার সময়ে দেখলাম গোঁসাই কুন্ডের জল পাথরের মধ্যে দিয়ে পশ্চিম দিকে আগের দেখা হ্রদটিতে গিয়ে পড়ছে। ঐ হ্রদটির নাম নাগকুন্ড। দেখলে কেমন গা ছমছম করে। চারিদিক পরিক্রমা করে এসে দেখলাম সেই আমেরিকান ত্রয়ী এসে পৌঁছালো। চারদিক কেমন শান্ত ছিল। ক্রমশঃ কোলাহল মুখর হয়ে উঠলো। বিকেলের দিকে দেখি আমার কালকের যাত্রা পথ ধরে একে একে কয়েকটি মূর্তি নেমে আসছে হ্রদের তীরবর্তী রাস্তায়। একে একে তারা লজে এসে পৌঁছালো। ছ'জনার দল। দু'জন তরুণ আর চারজন তরুণী। পরিশ্রান্ত শরীর। শুনলাম সকালে যাত্রা শুরু করেছে ঘোপ্তে থেকে। আমার কালকের গন্তব্য। প্রায় আট ন' ঘণ্টার পথ। এরা সব এসেছে সুইজারল্যান্ড থেকে। ছ'বন্ধু এসেছে এক সুন্দরের দেশ থেকে আর এক সুন্দরের দেশে। এরা লোক বেশ ভালো। আমার আমেরিকান সহযাত্রীদের মতো নয়। কথা বলে বেশ ভালো লাগলো। পরস্পর জেনে নিলাম কালকের পথের হদিশ। সন্ধ্যায় ফায়ারপ্লেসের চারিদিকে বসে খাওয়ার পালা সাঙ্গ করে আমি তাড়াতাড়ি শুতে চলে গেলাম বিদায় নিয়ে। কাল আমার পথের কঠিনতম অংশ এবং অজানাও বটে।

আজ ৩০শে সেপ্টেম্বর। আমার হাঁটা পথের চতুর্থ দিন। সকাল সাতটার মধ্যে ব্রেকফাস্ট খেয়ে বেড়িয়ে পড়লাম। গোঁসাই কুন্ডের ধার দিয়ে পথ উঠে গেছে পাসের দিকে । এখনো সূর্যের আলো এখানে এসে পড়েনি। ভোরের আলোয় নীল সরোবর নীল আকাশের প্রেক্ষাপটে অপূর্ব লাগছে। চোখের আড়াল হবার আগে শেষবারের মতো ছবি তুলে নিয়ে রাস্তার দিকে মন দিলাম। আবহাওয়া অত্যন্ত খারাপ। মাঝে মধ্যেই সূর্যালোক ঘন কুয়াশায় হারিয়ে যাচ্ছে। এতদিনকার প্রচলিত পথ এতক্ষণে শেষ হয়েছে। এখন পাহাড়ের ঢালে কেবল পাথরের রাজত্ব। তারই মধ্যে কোথাও পথরেখা আছে; কোথাও বা কেয়ার্ন করা রয়েছে। ওটাই পথের নির্দেশ। সাবধানে পথ চলেছি। একা, সম্পূর্ণ একা। কেমন ভয় ভয় লাগছে। এই ঘন কুয়াশার রাজত্বে পথ হারাবো না তো! কুয়াশা ঘন

হতেই সূর্যদেবের প্রার্থনা করছি। এইভাবে একসময় দেখি পথের বাঁ পাশে একটি মাঝারি আকারের সরোবর। ছবি নিলাম। কিন্তু মনে মনে সন্দেহ উঁকি দিচ্ছে ম্যাপে তো কোন সরোবরের চিহ্ন নেই। তাহলে কি পথ ভুল হলো! তবু এগিয়ে যাই। আপাদমস্তক আচ্ছাদিত তীব্র হাওয়ার প্রকোপ থেকে বাঁচতে। মনে মনে সূর্যের জন্য আকুল প্রার্থনা। একসময়ে কাঙ্খিত পাসটি হঠাৎ সামনে আসে। বুঝলাম পতাকা উড়তে দেখে। কয়েকটা অস্থায়ী দোকানের চিহ্ন। কুয়াশা কাটতেই মূহুর্তের মধ্যে দেখি পথের ডানদিকে অনতি দুরেই সূর্যকুন্ড। ওপারের পাহাড়ে বরফের আভাস। দু'মূহুর্ত দাঁড়িয়ে পকেট থেকে চকোলেট বার করে অজানা দেবতার উদ্দেশ্যে নিবেদন করি। তারপর আবার চলা শুরু। পথ এবার অকস্মাৎ ঢালু হয়ে নীচের দিকে নেমেছে। মনের মধ্যে এক অনির্বচনীয় আনন্দের চাপা উত্তেজনা। চলার গতি দ্রুত হলো। ঘড়িতে দেখি প্রায় ঘণ্টা দেড়েক হলো পথ হাঁটছি। হঠাৎই দেখি নীচের দিক থেকে এক পথিক মাথা নীচু করে চড়াই ভাঙছে। কাছে আসতেই আলিঙ্গন। যেন কতকালের চেনা বন্ধুর সঙ্গে হঠাৎ দেখা হয়ে গেছে। অথচ আমরা কেউ কাউকে আগে কোনোদিন দেখিনি আর ভবিষ্যতেও কোনদিন দেখা হবে না হয়তো। ও আসছে অস্ট্রিয়া থেকে। পাস পেরিয়ে ও যাবে গোঁসাই কুন্ড। আর পাস উত্তীর্ণ আমি যাবো ঘোপ্তে। পরস্পর শুভেচ্ছা ও পথের হদিশ বিনিময় করে আবার যে যার পথে। এক অদ্ভুত অনুভূতিতে মনটা ভরে গেল। দ্রুত পা চালালাম।। কিন্তু পথ তো গোঁসাই কুন্ডেই শেষ হয়েছে। এখন যা আছে তা' পথের চিহ্ন মাত্র। কোথাও কোথাও তার অবস্থা অকথ্য। প্রায় সাড়ে তিন ঘণ্টা চলার পর 'ফেদিতে' এসে পৌঁছালাম। 'ফেদি' কোন বিশেষ জায়গার নাম নয়। নেপালের প্রতিটা পাসের নীচে যে অস্থায়ী আস্তানা থাকে তাকেই 'ফেদি' বলে। এখানেও একটা মাত্র চায়ের দোকান। অবশ্য প্রয়োজনে থাকাও যায়। আমার অস্ট্রিয়ান বন্ধু এখান থেকেই ভোর ছ'টায় যাত্রা শুরু করেছিল। আমি খানিক বিশ্রাম নিয়ে, চা খেয়ে ঘোপ্তের উদ্দেশ্যে যাত্রা শুরু করলাম। জঙ্গল শুরু হলো। পথও পাল্লা দিয়ে খারাপ হতে শুরু করেছে। তারপর আবার চড়াই উৎরাই ও পর্যায়ক্রমে একঘেয়ে পাহাড়ের পর পাহাড় ডিঙোনো। আরো প্রায় আড়াই ঘণ্টা নিরবিচ্ছিন্ন চলার পর ধৈর্য্যের প্রায় শেষ প্রান্তে এসে পৌঁছালাম ঘোপ্তেতে। জঙ্গলের মধ্যেই একটুখানি পরিস্কার জায়গায় দুটো দোকান নিয়ে ঘোপ্তে। এসবই অস্থায়ী আস্তানা। সারাদিনে প্রায় ছ' ঘণ্টা চলেছি। ভীষন ক্লান্ত লাগছে। ডিম সেদ্ধ আর টম্যাটো স্যুপ খেয়ে তবে একটু চাঙ্গা লাগলো। রাতে শরীর খারাপ হয়েছিলো। জ্বর আর পেটের গন্ডগোল। সঙ্গে ওষুধ ছিল, খেলাম। পরদিন সকালে অবশ্য শরীরে আর জ্বর নেই। কিন্তু খুব সুস্থও নয়। তবু বেড়িয়ে পড়লাম। আজও লম্বা পথ পাড়ি দিতে হবে থারেয়াপত্তী হয়ে কুটুমসঙও।

দু' ঘন্টায় চলে এলাম থারেয়াপট্টী। মাসরুম স্যুপের অর্ডার দিয়ে ডিম সেদ্ধ নিয়ে বসলাম। যে পথ পেরিয়ে এসেছি তা' এক কথায় জঘন্য। এদের কাছেই জানলাম এইবার গ্রাম এসে গেছে বলে পথ আর অত খারাপ হবে না। থারেপট্টী জায়গাটা বেশ ভালো। এখানে কয়েকটা হোটেল আছে। কয়েকজনকে দেখলাম একটু ওপরের পথ দিয়ে যাচ্ছে মেলামচি গ্রামে। এই পথ হলো সুন্দরীজল থেকে শুরু করে আবার সুন্দরীজলেই শেষ। খাওয়া শেষ করে আবার চরৈবেতি, চরৈবেতি। দুপুরের পরে এক জায়গায় এসে দু'টো চায়ের দোকান কাম হোটেল পেলাম। এখানে একটা পুলিশ চৌকি আছে। বিদেশিদের এখানে অনুমতি পত্র দেখাতে হয়। চা খেয়ে আবার চলা আর চলা। জঙ্গলের মধ্যে দিয়ে চলেছি তো চলেইছি। পথ যেন আর শেষ হয় না। একসময় জঙ্গল একটু পাতলা হলো। অদুরে গ্রামের আভাস দেখে চলার গতি আপনিই বেড়ে গেল। আট ঘণ্টার পদচারণা অবশেষে শেষ হলো কুটুমসঙ গ্রামের এক সুন্দর হোটেলের দরজায়। দোতলার ঘরে স্যাক রেখে চা খেতে খেতে গ্রামটার চারিদিক দেখতে দেখতে সারাদিনের হাঁটার কথা ভাবছিলাম। যেন কতদিন পরে আবার লোকালয়ে এসে পৌঁছালাম। কুটুমসঙ গ্রামটি বেশ বর্ধিষ্ণু। এদিকে নেপালীদের বাস। ওপারের মতো তিব্বতিরা এদিকে অনুপস্থিত। এ গ্রামে বিদ্যুৎ আসেনি। কিন্তু টেলিফোনের লাইন রয়েছে। রয়েছে আই.এস.ডি. র সুবিধা । খানিক পরে নীচের দিক থেকে তরুণ তরুণী মিলিয়ে ছ'জনের একটা জার্মানির দল এলো। রাতে খেতে বসে আলাপ হলো। ওরা আমার কাছে পথের হদিশ জেনে নিল। আমি শেষের দিকে আর ওরা শুরুর পথে। আবহাওয়া বিকেল থেকেই খারাপ ছিল। রাতে যথারীতি বৃষ্টি হলো।

পরদিন নিয়মমাফিক ভোরে ওঠা। সবকিছু গুছিয়ে চা ব্রেকফাস্ট খেয়ে পথে নেমে পড়লাম। নেপালের হাঁটা পথের এই একটা সুবিধা। সব জায়গাতেই থাকা যায় আর প্রচুর বিদেশি পর্যটকদের দৌলতে বিভিন্ন ইউরোপীয়ান খাবার মেলে প্রায় প্রতিটি জায়গায়। আমার আজকের লক্ষ্য 'চিসাপানি'। কাগজেকলমে ছ' ঘণ্টার পথ। এ পথে কয়েকটা গ্রাম আছে। তাই পথের হালও অনেকটা ভালো হয়েছে। 'গুলভনজন' এ পৌঁছে দেখি বাড়ী বাড়ী পুজোর আয়োজন হচ্ছে। খেয়াল হলো আজ ২রা অক্টোবর, বিজয়া দশমী। এখানে দশেরার উৎসব আজ ও কাল দু'দিন ধরে। দুপুর নাগাদ পৌঁছালাম 'চিপলিং''। মাঝে বৃষ্টির জন্য কিছুক্ষণ থামতে হয়েছিল। এখানে নুডুল স্যুপ দিয়ে দুপুরের আহার সারলাম। কিছুক্ষণ বিশ্রাম নিয়ে আবার চলতে শুরু করলাম। সামনেই প্রায় হাজার ফুটের চড়াই ভাঙতে হবে। ধীরে ধীরে সেই কষ্টও শেষ হলো। বিকেল নাগাদ এসে পৌঁছালাম 'চিসাপানি'। একটা ঘর দখল করে এক প্রস্থ চা খেয়ে এদিক ওদিক ঘুরে দেখতে লাগলাম। বেশ

কয়েকজন বিদেশি ট্রেকারকেও দেখলাম। পথেও আজ অনেকগুলো দলের সঙ্গে দেখা হলো। সন্ধ্যার মুখে ঘন কুয়াশার মধ্যে হঠাৎ বাঙলা কথা শুনে এগিয়ে গিয়ে দেখি কোলকাতা থেকে ছ'জনের একটা দল এসে পৌঁছাল। এরা আজই বীরগঞ্জ থেকে কাঠমান্ডু ও সুন্দরীজল হয়ে এই সন্ধ্যায় এখানে এল। যাবে গৌঁসাই কুন্ড হয়ে ল্যাংট্যাং। ভাবছিলাম এরাও বেড়াতে এসেছে। অনেক দিন পরে বাঙলায় কথা বলে যে ভালোটা লাগছিলো সেটা কেমন মিইয়ে গেল। নিজের ঘরে এসে শুয়ে পড়লাম। আগামীকালই আমার হাঁটা পথের শেষ। আবার লোকালয়, কোলাহল, সেই পরিচিত শব্দ আর দৃশ্য। এইসব ভাবতে ভাবতে কখন ঘুমিয়ে পড়লাম।

পরদিন ভোরে উঠে যখন সব সেরে আমি পথে নামছি বাঙালি দলটা দেখলাম ছুটির মেজাজে। আমি তো নামবো, আর এরা উঠবে; কখন বেরোবে তাহলে? 'যাক্ গে!' বলে নিজের পথে এগিয়ে চলি। একটা চড়াই এর মাথায় উঠে পিছন ফিরে দেখি হিমালয়ের পুরো রেঞ্জ যাদের আমি কাছ থেকে দেখে এসেছি তারা সবাই দিগন্তে দাঁড়িয়ে আমায় যেন বিদায় জানাচ্ছে। মনে মনে সেই সুন্দরকে প্রণাম জানিয়ে একটা বাঁক ঘুরে নেমে চললাম নীচের দিকে। সুন্দর পথ। অনেকটা চলার পরে সুন্দরীজল গ্রামের আভাস। নীচে ছবির মতো ছড়ানো সমতল নজরে এলো। পথ গ্রামের মধ্যে দিয়ে বাঁধানো সিঁড়ি দিয়ে নেমে গেছে সোজা সুন্দরীজল নদীর বুকে। এখানে একটা জলবিদ্যুৎ প্রকল্প রয়েছে। জায়গাটা বেশ সুন্দর। খানিকক্ষণ বসতে ইচ্ছা হলো। বসে আছি, দেখি হল্যান্ড থেকে আগত এক ভদ্রলোক সঙ্গে স্ত্রী ও দুই কন্যা। কাছে আসতে আলাপ হলো। চারমাসের লম্বা ছুটিতে বিভিন্ন দেশ ভ্রমণে বেড়িয়েছেন। আমরা ভাবতেও পারিনা। নামতে নামতে এক সময়ে এসে পৌঁছালাম নীচে বাসস্ট্যান্ডে। বাস নেই। শেয়ার ট্যাক্সি নিয়ে গাড়ি বদল করে বেলা একটা নাগাদ কাঠমান্ডু। সন্ধ্যার বাসের টিকিট কেটে অপেক্ষা। এখন বাড়ি, স্ত্রী, পুত্র, পরিবার, পাড়া, অফিস সব যেন কত ভালো, কত প্রিয় বোধ হচ্ছে। এই ভালো লাগা এই পাহাড়ে, এই দুর্গমে না এলে টের পাই না। তাইতো বার বার পাহাড়ের কাছে আসি। বার বার আমাদের আসতে হয়।

*****

চেনা গন্তব্য হ'তে অচেনা পথে

আশিস মুখার্জী

নীল আকাশে শরতের মেঘের আনাগোনা শুরু হলেই মনটা কেমন উচাটন হয়ে যায় হিমালয়ের ডাকে। প্রতি বছরই আমি অন্তরে হিমালয়ের এই আহ্বান অনুভব করি। অগত্যা সে বছর ঠিক হলো পিন্ডারি গ্লেসিয়ার। আরে এতো চেনা পথ, পরিচিত গন্তব্য। তাহলে নামকরণের সার্থকতা কোথায়? সেই ক্লাইম্যাক্সে পৌঁছাতে গেলে পাঠককে একটু ধৈর্য ধরে পড়তে হবে গন্তব্যের শেষ কোথায়। অসমবয়সী সঙ্গী ঠিক হলো আমার অফিসেরই তিন সহকর্মী বন্ধু। বলাইদা, আমাদের দলের সর্বজ্যেষ্ঠ্য, উজ্জ্বলদা বিখ্যাত পর্বতারোহী,স্বপনদা ও আমি সর্বকনিষ্ঠ। গন্তব্য হিসেবে পিন্ডারি গ্লেসিয়ার নির্বাচন করার অন্যতম কারণ হলো এ পথের সহজগম্যতা এবং পথের সর্বত্র ফরেষ্ট বাংলোর সুবিধা। ফলতঃ কেদার বদ্রীর তীর্থযাত্রী বাদ দিলে পিন্ডারি ও আমাদের পশ্চিমবঙ্গের সান্দাকফুতেই সবচেয়ে বেশি সংখ্যক পদযাত্রীর সমাগম ঘটে। যথাসময়ে আমরা সবাই হাওড়া ষ্টেশনে মিলিত হলাম। ফার্ষ্ট ক্লাস ক্যুপে আমাদের চারটে বার্থ। দারুন ব্যাপার! একটা ঘরে নিরুপদ্রব যাত্রা। যথাসময়ে ট্রেন ছাড়লো। আমাদের প্রাথমিক গন্তব্য লখনৌ। তখন কুমায়ুনের নৈনিতাল,আলমোরা যেতে হলে লখনৌ থেকে মিটার গেজের লাইনের জন্য ট্রেন বদল করতে হতো। একান্ত নিজস্ব ক্যুপের মধ্যে অগাধ স্বাধীনতা আর উজ্জ্বলদার বিভিন্ন পর্বত অভিযানের কাহিনী উপভোগ করতে করতে আমাদের যাত্রাপর্বের সূচনা হলো।

পরদিন সকালে ট্রেন লখনৌ পৌঁছালো যথারীতি খানিক বিলম্বে। আমাদেরও তাড়া নেই। কাঠগোদাম এক্সপ্রেস ছাড়বে রাত ন'টা নাগাদ। অতএব লকার রুমে আমাদের ব্যাগপত্র রেখে আমরা বের হলাম শহরটা ঘুরে দেখতে। লখনৌ প্রাচীন ঐতিহাসিক শহর। কাজেই বহু ঐতিহাসিক দ্রষ্টব্য এখানকার বিশেষ আকর্ষণ। আমরা একটা ট্যাক্সি ভাড়া করে বেরিয়ে পড়লাম। দ্বিপ্রাহরিক আহার সেরে একেবারে সন্ধ্যার মুখে ফিরে এলাম। সঙ্গে রইল ট্রেনে রাতে খাবার জন্য কিছু আহার্য। ছোট লাইনের প্লাটফর্ম থেকে রাতের ট্রেন যথাসময়ে ছাড়লো। ট্রেনের কামরা প্রস্থে ছোট হলেও বেশ পরিচ্ছন্ন। পরদিন সকালে যথাসময়ে ট্রেন পৌঁছালো কাঠগোদাম। আমরা ষ্টেশনের বাইরে এসে খোঁজ করলাম বাসের। আমাদের গন্তব্য ভারারি নামে একটি ছোট্ট জনপদ। বাসের টিকিট কেটে আমাদের মালপত্র রেখে আমরা সামান্য চা জলখাবার খেয়ে এসে বসলাম। বাস চলতে শুরু করল, বাগেশ্বর

হয়ে যাবে ভারারি। বাগেশ্বরে ক্ষণিক বিরতি। সরযূ ও গোমতী নদীর সঙ্গমস্থল। দুপুর পেরিয়ে যাবার পর আমরা আমাদের গন্তব্যে এসে পৌঁছলাম। কাছেই একটা থাকা খাওয়ার আস্তানা জুটলো। ঘর বেশ পরিস্কার। ঘরে আমাদের জিনিসপত্র রেখে আমরা বাইরে এলাম চারপাশটা একটু ঘুরে দেখবার জন্য। জানা গেল লোহারক্ষেত পর্যন্ত ছোট গাড়ি যায়। দূরত্ব এগারো কিলোমিটার। খবর ভালোই। তাহলে অন্তত কিছুটা পথ এগিয়ে যেতে পারলে আমাদের প্রথম রাত ঢাকুরি বাংলোয় কাটাতে কোনো অসুবিধা হবে না।

কিন্তু বিধি বাম। পরদিন প্রাতে হোটেলের খরচাপাতি মিটিয়ে চা খেয়ে যখন পথে নামলাম তখন কোন গাড়ির দেখা নেই। অগত্যা চরৈবেতি। ঘণ্টা তিনেকেই পৌঁছে গেলাম লোহারক্ষেত বনবাংলোয়। ঘড়িতে বেলা এগারোটা মোটে। একপ্রস্থ চা পানের পর ঠিক হলো আমরা দুপুরের খাবার প্যাক করে নিয়ে ঢাকুরির উদ্দেশ্যে রওনা হবো। পথ তো আর মাত্র দশ কিলোমিটার। বিকেলের মধ্যেই ঠিক পৌঁছে যাবো। এইখানেই হলো প্রথম ভুল। কেননা দলে বয়স্ক এবং অনভিজ্ঞ সদস্য আছে। সঙ্গে আছে ঢাকুরি পাসের বিখ্যাত চড়াই। কাজেই যতই বেলা বাড়তে লাগলো ততই দলের গতি মন্থর হতে লাগলো। অবশেষে আমরা যখন ঢাকুরি টপে পৌঁছালাম তখন সূর্য পাটে গেছেন। আকাশে কেবল পড়ন্ত বিকেলের ম্লান আলোটুকু লেগে আছে। ঢাকুরি বাংলো চত্বরের আভাসটুকু এখান থেকে পাওয়া যায়। কিন্তু বেশ বুঝতে পারছি আসন্ন সন্ধ্যায় জঙ্গলের মধ্যে দিয়ে বাকি পথটুকু যেতে রাত হয়ে যাবে। কিন্তু থামার কোন প্রশ্নই নেই। সামনে ঢাকুরি বাংলোর নিশ্চিন্ত আশ্রয়,লেপের ওম আমাদের হাতছানি দিয়ে ডাকছে। বলাইদা আর স্বপনদাকে সেই আহ্বানে উৎসাহ দিলাম। উজ্জ্বলদা নির্বিকার। সবাই এবার একসঙ্গে পথ চলছি। কিন্তু দিনের শেষে গতি বড় ধীর। সন্ধ্যা সাতটা নাগাদ যখন ঢাকুরি বাংলোয় পৌঁছালাম তখন আর কারো মুখেই কোন কথা নেই। আমি চৌকিদারকে খুঁজে ডেকে আনলাম। ও এই অসময়ে আমাদের চারজনকে দেখে একটু অবাকই হল। তাড়াতাড়ি আমাদের একটা ঘর খুলে দিয়েই ও গেল চায়ের ব্যবস্থা করতে। কিছুক্ষণের মধ্যেই গরম চা ও সঙ্গে আনা বিস্কুট সেবনের পর সবাই একটু ধাতস্থ হলো। চৌকিদারকে বললাম রাতের খাবারের যা হোক একটা ব্যবস্থা করতে। আমরা বিছানায় যে যার মতো গুছিয়ে বসেছি। ঘড়িতে এখন প্রায় রাত আটটা। অন্যান্য ঘরের যাত্রীরা মনে হয় এখন রাতের খাবার খেয়ে শোবার তোড়জোড় করছে। বুঝতে পারছি প্রথম দিনেই একটানা এগারো ঘণ্টা ধরে প্রায় একুশ কিলোমিটার হাঁটার ধকল বলাইদা আর স্বপনদার ওপর একটু বেশিই প্রভাব ফেলেছে। যাইহোক ঐ

প্রসঙ্গ আর তুললাম না। ইতিমধ্যেই চৌকিদার চারটে প্লেটে গরম খিচুড়ি নিয়ে এসেছে। কাজেই তার সদ্ব্যবহার করে লেপের মধ্যে ঢুকতে বেশি সময় লাগলো না।

পরদিন ঘুম ভাঙ্গলো চৌকিদারের ডাকে। গরম চায়ের কাপ নিয়ে সে আমাদের ঘুম ভাঙ্গালো আমারই পূর্ব নির্দেশ মতো। বিছানায় বসেই আমরা চায়ের কাপ হাতে তুলে নিলাম। আর তখনই বলাইদা প্রথম বোমাটা ফাটালেন। "আশিস, আমার পায়ের অবস্থা ভালো নয়। আমি এখানেই থেকে যাই। তোরা বরং ঘুরে আয়।" আমরা যখন একথা শুনে পরস্পর মুখ চাওয়া চাওয়ি করছি তখনই দ্বিতীয় তোপটা দাগলো স্বপনদা, "বলাইদা যদি থেকে যায় তাহলে আমিও বলাইদার সঙ্গে থেকে যাই। আমারও পায়ের অবস্থা ভালো নয়।" এর অর্থ হলো আমাদের চারজনের দল এখন দ্বিধা বিভক্ত। আমি আর উজ্জ্বলদা যেতে সক্ষম। আর বলাইদা ও স্বপনদা যেতে অপারগ। এমতাবস্থায় আমি কিংকর্তব্যবিমূঢ় হয়ে উজ্জ্বলদার দিকে তাকালাম। শেষমেশ উজ্জ্বলদা ও বলাইদার সমঝোতায় ঠিক হলো আমি আর উজ্জ্বলদা আমাদের পূর্ব নির্ধারিত গন্তব্যের দিকে এগোবো আর বলাইদা ও স্বপনদা ঢাকুরিতে একদিন বিশ্রাম নিয়ে তারপর ফেরার পথ ধরবে এবং আমরা মিলিত হবো নৈনিতালে।। বলাইদাদের দোষ দেওয়া যায় না। ট্রেকিং এর প্রথম দিনেই যদি এগারো ঘণ্টা ধরে হেঁটে একুশ কিলোমিটার পথ পাড়ি দিতে হয় তাহলে কারো কারো শরীর না বলতেই পারে।

অতঃপর আমি আর উজ্জ্বলদা তাড়াতাড়ি আমাদের রুকস্যাক গুছিয়ে নিয়ে পথে নামলাম। বলাইদা আর স্বপনদা আমাদের শুভযাত্রা কামনা করে হাসিমুখে বিদায় জানালেন। সহজ সরল পথে আমরা খানিক দ্রুতই পরবর্তী গ্রাম খাতি পৌঁছে গেলাম। ঘড়িতে বেলা এগারোটা। এখানে দুপুরের আহার সারতে সারতে ঠিক হলো আমরা যত দ্রুত সম্ভব আমাদের যাত্রা শেষ করবো যাতে করে আমরা খুব তাড়াতাড়ি বলাইদাদের সঙ্গে আবার মিলিত হতে পারি। স্থানীয় বাংলো সন্নিহিত দোকানে আমরা আহার শেষ করে আবার পথে নামলাম। লক্ষ্য পরবর্তী জনপদ দাওলি পেরিয়ে ফুরকিয়া বাংলোয় রাত্রিবাস। ঢাকুরি থেকে দূরত্ব প্রায় ছাব্বিশ কিলোমিটার। আমারা আট কিলোমিটার পেরিয়ে এসেছি আর হাতে সময়ও আছে যথেষ্ট। অতএব আমরা দুই বন্ধু আবার পথে নামলাম এবং বিরতিহীন পথ চলে এসে উপস্থিত হলাম দাওলি বনবিশ্রামগৃহে। চা পানের বিরতি। হাতে এখনও যথেষ্ট সময় আছে। অতএব পারিপার্শ্বিক এখন নিশ্চিন্তে উপভোগ করা যায়। ডানদিক থেকে নেমে এসেছে কাফনি গ্লেসিয়ার থেকে কাফনি নালা। ছোট্ট কিন্তু উচ্ছল নদী এসে মিলিত হয়েছে পিন্ডার গঙ্গার সঙ্গে। প্রসঙ্গত উল্লেখ্য পিন্ডার গঙ্গার নামটা

এসেছে সেই মহাভারত থেকেই। পান্ডবরা নাকি এখানে পিন্ড দান করেই বাণপ্রস্থের পথে পাড়ি দিয়ে ছিলেন। আর কাফনি নালা ধরে যাওয়া যায় কাফনি গ্লেসিয়ার। অভিযাত্রীর প্রস্তুতি থাকলে কাফনি গ্লেসিয়ার পেরিয়ে পৌঁছানো যায় নামিক গ্লেসিয়ার যেখান থেকে সৃষ্টি হয়েছে রামগঙ্গা নদী। যাইহোক আমাদের এখনো প্রায় সাত কিলোমিটার পথ পাড়ি দিতে হবে। অতএব বিলম্ব না করে আমারা আবার পথে নামলাম। এ পথে খাতির পরে আর গ্রাম নেই। কাজেই বনবাংলোর চৌকিদারই ভরসা। আমাদের যাত্রা সঙ্গী পিন্ডারি নদী এখানে উচ্ছল এবং আমাদের পাশে পাশে নিজস্ব ছন্দে বয়ে চলেছে অলকানন্দার সঙ্গে মিলিত হবার জন্য। নীচে তার নাম কর্ণগঙ্গা। আর সংগমস্থলের নাম কর্ণপ্রয়াগ। ক্রমশঃ বড় গাছপালা কমে আসতে শুরু করলো। বুঝলাম আমরা ট্রীলাইনের উপরে উঠে এসেছি। অবশেষে এক জনবিরল পথ প্রান্তে ফুরকিয়া বাংলোর দেখা পেলাম। রাতের আশ্রয় নজরে আসতেই চলার গতি বাড়লো। আমরা বিকেলের আলো থাকতেই পৌঁছে গেলাম ফুরকিয়া বাংলোর উষ্ণ আশ্রয়ে। বিশাল হলঘরের এক প্রান্তে আমাদের ম্যাট্রেস পেতে রুকস্যাক রেখে বেরিয়ে এলাম বাইরে। হাতে গরম চায়ের কাপ। কিন্তু বেশিক্ষণ থাকা গেল না। নদীখাত থেকে ছুটে আসা তীব্র হাওয়া আমাদের ঘরে ঢুকিয়ে দিল। ঘরে আরো অনেক যাত্রী রয়েছে। তবে কোন বিশৃঙ্খলা নেই।। সন্ধ্যার কিছু পরেই রাতের খাওয়া সাঙ্গ হল। স্লীপিং ব্যাগের মধ্যে আশ্রয় নিলাম। কেননা ভোর রাত তিনটের সময়ে আমাদের যাত্রা শুরু করতে হবে পিন্ডারি নদীর উৎস মুখের উদ্দেশ্যে। দূরত্ব প্রায় সাত কিলোমিটার।

এলার্মের ব্যবস্থা ছিল না। কিন্তু সহযাত্রীদের কলস্বরে ঘুম ভেঙে গেল। অনেক কষ্টে স্লীপিং ব্যাগের ওম ছেড়ে বেরিয়ে ধরাচূড়া পরে যখন পথে নামলাম ঘড়িতে তখন রাত তিনটে বেজে গেছে। পথ অন্ধকার, আকাশ নক্ষত্র খচিত। টর্চের আলোয় আমরা কয়েকজন প্রাণী নির্বাক হয়ে পথ চলেছি। একমাত্র অনতিদূরে নদীর কলস্বর ভিন্ন কোন শব্দ নেই। চারিদিকে এক অদ্‌ভুত নৈঃশব্দ্য বিরাজ করছে। ক্রমশঃ আকাশ পরিষ্কার হলো প্রাক সূর্যোদয়ের আভায়। আমাদের পথের পারিপার্শ্বের একটা আভাস পাওয়া গেল। অনতিদূরে তুষার শুভ্র পর্বত চূড়া যেন ধ্যানমগ্ন। নদীর বিপরীত দিকে মাইকতোলি, সুন্দরদুঙ্গা অঞ্চলের পর্বত প্রাচীর। সামনে নন্দাখাত ও ছাংগোছ শীর্ষ। তারই মাঝ বরাবর এক তুষার নদী নেমে এসেছে। ঐতো পিন্ডারি গ্লেসিয়ার! হ্যাঁ, আমরা পিন্ডারি জিরো পয়েন্টে এসে গেছি। এপারে এখনো আবছায়া, কিন্তু ওপারে পাহাড়ের তুষার মুকুটে ভোরের প্রথম সূর্যকিরণের পরশ রঙের খেলায় মেতেছে। কখন আমাদের পা থেমে গেছে। আমরা নির্বাক বিস্ময়ে এই বিশাল প্রকৃতির প্রাঙ্গণে নিতান্ত কয়েকটি অকিঞ্চিৎকর

প্রাণী সম্মোহিত হয়ে দাঁড়িয়ে আছি। প্রথমে গোলাপী তারপর সোনালী হয়ে যখন রূপোর মতো সামনের পর্বতশীর্ষ আর বরফ নদী ঝকঝক করে উঠলো তখন আমাদের দৃষ্টি গোচর হল সেই বরফ নদী যা বিখ্যাত ট্রেলস্ পাস থেকে পাঁচ হাজার ফুট নেমে এসেছে। ১৮৩০ সালে কুমায়ুনের প্রথম কমিশনার ট্রেল সাহেব এই পথে পিন্ডার উপত্যকা থেকে মিলাম উপত্যকা গিয়েছিলেন। তাঁর নামানুসারে এই গিরিপথের নাম হয় "ট্রেলস পাস"। তাঁর সেই যাত্রায় সঙ্গী হয়েছিলেন মালিক সিং বুদার নামে এক স্থানীয় ব্যক্তি। ১৭৭০০ ফুট উঁচু এই গিরিপথ বহু ভারতীয় এবং বিদেশি অভিযাত্রী দল অতিক্রম করার চেষ্টা করেন। কিন্তু কেউই সফল হননি। তবে ১৯৭২ সালে পশ্চিমবঙ্গ থেকে একটি অভিযাত্রী দল পিন্ডারির দিক থেকে এই গিরিপথ অতিক্রম করার চেষ্টা করেন। তাঁরা চারটে ক্যাম্প করে গিরিপথ শীর্ষে পৌঁছাতে সক্ষম হন। কিন্তু বরফের অবস্থা খারাপ থাকায় এবং কোনো ভারবাহক রাজী না হওয়ায় তারা বিঠলগোয়ার নামার আশা ত্যাগ করে একই পথে ফিরে আসেন। এই আপাত ব্যর্থ অভিযানগুলোই বুঝিয়ে দেয় যে "ট্রেলস পাস" আজকাল আর শুধু ট্রেকার্সদের জন্য নয় পর্বত অভিযাত্রীদের কাছেও বেশ দূর্লঙ্ঘনীয়।

এতক্ষণে পাহাড়ের প্রাচীর ডিঙিয়ে এপারেও সূর্যালোক এসে পড়েছে। আমারও এবার ফেরার পথ ধরলাম। এবার খানিকটা আসার পর নজরে এলে এক বিরাট পাথরের ওভারহ্যাংএর নীচে এক সাধুর কুঠির। যাবার সময়ে অন্ধকারে লক্ষ্য করিনি। সাধুবাবার বয়স বেশি নয়। এই নির্জন প্রান্তরে একা কুঠির বানিয়ে তপস্যায় রত। শীতকালে নীচে নেমে যাবেন। আমরা ক্ষণিক বিশ্রামের জন্য ওনার আশ্রয়ে থামলাম। উনি দুটি গ্লাসে আমাদের চা এগিয়ে দিলেন। ধুনির আগুনের তাপ আর গরম চা অযাচিত ভাবে পাওয়ায় আমরা আমাদের আন্তরিক কৃতজ্ঞতা জানাতে উনি খুব স্বাভাবিক ভাবেই তা' গ্রহণ করলেন। যেন এটা তেমন কোন ব্যাপারই নয়। খানিকক্ষণ পরে আমরা প্রণাম করে দক্ষিণা দিতে চাইলে উনি তা' সবিনয়ে প্রত্যাখ্যান করে আমাদের আশীর্বাদ করলেন। আমরা দ্রুত পায়ে এবার ফেরার পথ ধরলাম। ঘন্টা দু'য়েকের মধ্যেই আমরা ফুরকিয়া বাংলোয় হাজির হলাম। চৌকিদারকে তার পাওনা গন্ডা মিটিয়ে আমাদের রুকস্যাক উঠিয়ে আমরা আবার খাতির পথ ধরলাম। বিরতিহীন পথ চলে আমারা খাতি বনবাংলোয় এসে উপস্থিত হলাম। ঘড়িতে তখন বেলা এগারোটা। সংলগ্ন দোকানে খাবারের অর্ডার দিয়ে রুকস্যাক রেখে আমরা বাংলোর হাতায় যখন অপেক্ষা করছি তখনই নজরে পড়ল দোকানের দরজার পাশে একটা বোর্ডে এই অঞ্চলের ট্রেকিং রুট গুলির একটা হাতে আঁকা ম্যাপ। তাতে সুন্দদুঙ্গা, পিন্ডারি,কাফনি, মিলাম সব জায়গার একটা পথরেখা এবং নির্দেশ দেওয়া আছে। কিন্তু যেটা আমার নজর কাড়লো সেটা হলো খাতি বনবাংলো থেকে একটা পথরেখা গিয়েছে ঢাকুরি

অর্থাৎ যে পথে আমরা এসেছি আর একটা পথ সোজা "খাতি খাল" অর্থাৎ খাতি পাস পেরিয়ে "সং"' গ্রামের দিকে। অর্থাৎ আমরা যদি সেই পথে যাই তাহলে আজই পৌঁছতে পারবো "সং" গ্রামে অর্থাৎ বাস রাস্তায়। এবং কালই ওখান থেকে বাস পেয়ে যাবো নৈনিতালের। আমাদের একদিন সাশ্রয় হবে। উজ্জ্বলদার দৃষ্টি আকর্ষণ করে বললাম,"দেখুন উজ্জ্বলদা,এই পথে যাবেন নাকি? নতুন পথে যাত্রা করাও হবে আর একটা দিন সাশ্রয়ও হবে। তাহলে আমাদের বলাইদাদের সঙ্গে পথেই হয়তো দেখা হয়ে যাবে।" উজ্জ্বলদা তৎক্ষণাৎ রাজি। বললেন,"তাহলে আগে পেট ভরে খেয়ে নাও। অজানা পথ আর কিছু নাও পেতে পারো।" খেতে খেতে আমি দোকানি কাম্ চৌকিদারকে একবার জিজ্ঞাসা করলাম ঐ পথের ব্যাপারে। চৌকিদার উৎসাহ দিয়ে বলল "আরে সাব, আপ যাইয়ে না। আপলোগ আজ হি "সং" পৌঁছ্ যাওগে। স্রিফ আপকো খাতি খালসে উতারনে কে বাদ ডাইনা বালা রাস্তা লেনে পড়েগা। উয়ো রাস্তা "স"' গাঁও যায়েগা। অউর বাঁয়ে বালা রাস্তা যাতা হ্যায় "কালঝুনি" গাঁও।" মনের মধ্যে একটা উত্তেজনা টের পাচ্ছি। এমন সময়ে ঘরে একজন যুবক প্রবেশ করলো। একে আমরা দেখেছি বাইরে রোদে শুয়ে বিশ্রাম করছিল। আমরা ভেবেছিলাম হয় পিন্ডারি যাবে কিংবা ফিরছে। আমরা অহেতুক কৌতুহল দেখাইনি। এখন ছেলেটি বিনা ভূমিকায় হঠাৎ আমাদের বলে বসলো," দাদা, আপলোগ নীচে যা রহা হ্যায় না? হামকো ভি মেহেরবানি করকে আপনা সাথ লে চলিয়ে না।" উজ্জ্বলদার দিকে তাকালাম। উজ্জ্বলদা বললেন "চলুক না।" "কিন্তু আমরা তো অন্য পথ দিয়ে ফিরবো।" আমার কথায় উজ্জ্বলদা বললেন "ঠিক আছে। এতদূর এসেছে যখন তখন ঠিক ফিরতে পারবে।" অতএব দু'জনের দল এখন তিন জন হলো। কথায় কথায় জানা গেল ছেলেটি দিল্লিতে থাকে। কয়েকজন বন্ধু মিলে এসেছিল পিন্ডারি যাবে বলে। ওর শরীর খারাপ বোধ করায় ও খাতিতে রয়ে গেছে। আর ওর বন্ধুরা গেছে এগিয়ে। যাইহোক ঘড়িতে সাড়ে বারোটা বেজে গেছে। আমরা আর দেরি না করে উঠে পড়লাম।

প্রচলিত পথ ছেড়ে শুরু হলো জঙ্গল আর চড়াই ভেঙে আমাদের অজানা পথে যাত্রা। পথ বলতে কিছু নেই। জঙ্গলের মধ্যে দিয়ে একটা পথরেখা সোজা উঠে গেছে পাহাড়ের ঢাল বেয়ে। মাঝে মাঝে থেমে উপরের দিকে তাকাই। কিন্তু বিশাল বিশাল গাছের মাথায ছাড়া আর কিছু চোখে পড়ে না। আমি একটু এগিয়ে আর ওরা দুজন পেছনে। বেশ খানিকটা যাবার পর একটা ভেড়াওয়ালাদের অস্থায়ী ছাউনী চোখে পড়লো। চারপাশটা বেশ পরিস্কার। একটু জিরিয়ে নেবার জন্য ক্ষনিক বিরতি। উজ্জ্বলদারা এসে পৌঁছালে জল খাওয়া হলো। পকেট থেকে ক্যাডবেরী বের করে সবাই মিলে ভাগ করে নিলাম। ঘড়িতে সাড়ে তিনটে বেজে গেছে। জানিনা এখনো কতটা পথ

পেরোলে পরে রাতের আশ্রয় পাবো। আমিই তাড়া লাগালাম। শুরু হলো আবার চড়াই ভাঙ্গা। হঠাৎ মনে হল আকাশ দেখা যাচ্ছে। ঠিকই তো, জঙ্গল এখানে অনেক পাতলা হয়ে এসেছে আর সত্যিই আমার সামনের দিকে পাহাড়ের প্রাচীরের ওপর দিয়ে আকাশ দেখা যাচ্ছে। অর্থাৎ আমি পাসের কাছাকাছি চলে এসেছি। আমর সব আশাকে সার্থক করে হঠাৎ সেই প্রাচীরের ওপর আবির্ভূত হলো চারটি মনুষ্য মূর্তি। দুজন পুরুষ ও দুজন রমণী পাসের বিপরীত দিক থেকে উঠে এসেছে। আমি যত বেশি আশ্চর্য হলাম তার চেয়েও বেশি বোধ হয় ওরা হয়েছে। ওরা স্থানীয় লোকজন। আমি বিদেশী। প্রচলিত পথ ছেড়ে এই অপ্রচলিত পথে কোন ভীনদেশী তো আসে না। পাসের ওপরেই আলাপ হলো। ওরা আসছে "কালঝুনি" গ্রাম থেকে। যাবে খাতি। আমাকে আবার বলে দিল ডানদিকের পথ ধরতে। আমি ওদের ধন্যবাদ জানিয়ে একটু বসলাম উজ্জ্বলদাদের আপেক্ষায়। নতুন ছেলেটি যোগদান করায় উজ্জ্বলদার গতি স্বাভাবিকভাবেই অনেক মন্থর হয়েছে। বেলা পড়ে এসেছে। ঘড়িতে সাড়ে চারটে বেজে গেছে। ওরা পাসের ওপর এসে পৌঁছাতেই আমি তাড়া লাগালাম। এখানেও ঢাকুরি পাসের মতো নিশান লাগানো। অদৃশ্য দেবতার প্রতি প্রণাম জানিয়ে আমরা নামতে শুরু করলাম। খানিকটা পথ নেমে আসার পর পথ দু'ভাগ হয়েছে। আমরা নির্দেশ মতো ডানদিকের পথ ধরলাম। আরো খানিকটা নামার পর পথ আশ্রয় নিয়েছে একটা শীর্ণ ঝর্ণার বুকে। শুরু হলো দূরন্ত উৎরাই। কখনো ছয় ইঞ্চি তো কখনো এক ফুট পাথরের ওপরে পা দিয়ে দেহের ভারসাম্য সামলে ঝর্ণাধারার সঙ্গে সঙ্গে নামা। ছোট্ট ঝর্ণাটি নীচে একটি পাহাড়ি নদীর সঙ্গে মিলিত হয়েছে। এখানে দুটো কাঠের গুঁড়ি ফেলা রয়েছে। সাবধানে সাঁকো পেরিয়ে এসে দাঁড়াই। উজ্জ্বলদারাও সাবধানে নেমে আসে। সন্ধ্যা ঘনিয়ে এসেছে। পথ এখন অনেক সমান্তরাল। দূরে গ্রামের আলোর আভাস দেখা যাচ্ছে। একসঙ্গে পথ চলতে থাকি ভাল্লুকের ভয়ে। ক্রমশঃ অন্ধকার গাঢ় হয়ে আসে। দূরে গ্রামের যে আলোর বিন্দুগুলো দেখা যাচ্ছিল, আমরা যত এগোই তারাও যেন ততই পিছিয়ে যায়। টর্চের আলোয় পথ চলি একসঙ্গে। সাড়ে ছ'টা বেজে গেল এইটুকু পথ নামতে। অদূরে একটা আলোর উৎস লক্ষ্য করে এগিয়ে চলি। আলোর উৎসের কাছে আসতে দেখি চারিদিকে উঁচু পাথরের পাঁচিল দেওয়া একটা পাথরের দ্বিতল বাড়ি। পথের সমান্তরালে একটা ঘর আর নীচের দিকে একটা ঘর। সেই ঘরের চারিপাশে উঁচু পাথরের পাঁচিল। ভেতরে উঠোনের মতো জায়গায় একপাল ভেড়া। ওপরেই ঘরের দাওয়ায় দু'জনের সঙ্গে দেখা হয়ে গেল। জানা গেল তারা আজই এসেছে খাতি থেকে। শীতের সময়ে এখন তারা নীচে নেমে যাবে। আমরা নিছকই ভ্রমণের উদ্দেশ্যে এসেছি শুনে তারা অতিথিবৎসল গৃহস্থের মত সাহায্যের হাত বাড়িয়ে দিল।

পাঁচ মিনিটের মধ্যেই গরম চায়ের গ্লাস হাতে দেখছি ওরা আমাদের থাকার জন্য সেই পাথরের চাতালে রাস্তার পাশেই তাঁবু টাঙাচ্ছে। আর অন্য জন রান্নার আয়োজনে ব্যস্ত। ভাবাই যায় না অনাহুত অতিথির জন্য এতো আয়োজন। আসলে এখানকার মানুষজনই এইরকম। আমরা অভিজ্ঞতা বলে এখানেই আসল ভারতবর্ষের সন্ধান পাওয়া যায়। ইতিপূর্বে এক মজাদার ঘটনা ঘটে গেছে যার জন্যই এই তাঁবুর আয়োজন। ওরা প্রথমে বলেছিল ওরা তো বাইরেই শোবে খোলা আকাশের নীচে। তবে নীচের ঘরটা যেটা ওরা গুদাম ঘর হিসেবে ব্যবহার করে সেখানে আমরা থাকতে পারি। উজ্জ্বলদা বললেন, "তাহলে আমরাও খোলা আকাশের নীচে পাথরের চাতালে থাকতে পারি। আমাদের তো স্লিপিং ব্যাগ, ম্যাট্রেস সবই আছে।" কিন্তু আমি জিজ্ঞেস করলাম,"তোমরা খোলা আকাশের নীচে কেন রাতে থাকবে?" তাঁর উত্তরে যা বললো তাতে আর আমাদের কারোরই অ্যাডভেঞ্চার করার ইচ্ছে রইল না। শুনলাম রাতে নাকি প্রায়ই শের আসে ভেড়ার লোভে। আর ভেড়া পাহারা দেবার জন্যই নাকি ওদের বাইরে শুতে হয়। কেননা ওদের সঙ্গে কোনো কুকুর নেই যা সাধারণত পাহারার কাজ করে থাকে। এই কথা শোনার পর উজ্জ্বলদাই প্রথম বললেন "আশিস, তুমি গিয়ে বরং একবার নীচের তলার ঘরটা দেখে এস। একটা রাত্তির, আমরা বরং ওখানেই শুয়ে যাবো।" কিন্তু আমি সরেজমিনে দেখে এসে বললাম, "উজ্জ্বলদা, চতুস্পদ প্রাণী ভিন্ন ওখানে থাকা সম্ভব নয়।" শেষমেশ ঠিক হলো আমরাও বাইরে ঐ চাতালেই শোবো। আর তাই শহুরে বাবুদের জন্য ঐ তাঁবুর আয়োজন। খাওয়া দাওয়া পর আমরা যখন শোবার আয়োজন করছি তখনো উজ্জ্বলদা বললেন, "আশিস, আমি বরং মাঝখানেই শুয়ে পড়ছি।" আমি আর কিছু বললাম না। শুধু নিজের মনেই হাসলাম।

পরদিন ভোরে উঠে আমরা এক প্রস্থ চা পানের পর ভেড়াওয়ালাদের আতিথেয়তার মান স্বরূপ আমাদের শহুরে শিক্ষায় কিছু মূল্য দিতে গিয়ে নিজেরাই অত্যন্ত অপ্রস্তুত হলাম। কেননা কাল রাতের আয়োজন ওরা কোনো বাণিজ্যিক দৃষ্টিভঙ্গি থেকে করেনি। ওরা ব্যবসায়ী নয়। আর এইটা ওদের পেশাও নয়। কাজেই অতিথি সৎকারের কোন মূল্য ওরা নিতে পারবে না। ক্ষুদ্র মনের মানুষ আমরা ওদের মন খুলে কৃতজ্ঞতা ও ধন্যবাদ জানিয়ে বিদায় নিলাম "সং" গ্রামের পথে। প্রকৃতপক্ষে আমরা গতরাতে "সং" গ্রামের প্রান্তেই এসে উপস্থিত হয়েছিলাম। তাই ঘন্টা খানেকের মধ্যেই আমরা গ্রামের বাসরাস্তায় এসে উপস্থিত হলাম। কিছুক্ষণের মধ্যেই আটটা নাগাদ ভারারি থেকে ছাড়া বাস এসে উপস্থিত হলো। আমরাও উঠে পড়লাম নৈনিতাল গামী বাসে। আর বাসে উঠেই সবচেয়ে বড় চমক। স্বপনদা হঠাৎ চেঁচিয়ে উঠলো বাসের পিছনের সিট থেকে, "আরে! আশিস, উজ্জ্বলদা! তোমরা কোথা

থেকে?" অযাচিত ভাবে আমাদের ভেঙে যাওয়া দলের চারজন আবার মিলিত হওয়ায় সবাই অত্যন্ত খুশি। আমরা নৈনিতাল পৌঁছাবার আগেই আবার একসঙ্গে মিলিত হতে পারলাম। এরপর পূর্ব নির্ধারিত সময়সূচি অনুযায়ী চেনা গন্তব্য। অর্থাৎ নৈনিতালে দুদিন বিরতি নিয়ে আবার যথারীতি লখনৌ হয়ে হাওড়া স্টেশন এবং যে যার বাড়ি নির্দিষ্ট দিনে।

কিন্তু এপর্যন্ত আপাত সরল ভ্রমণ কাহিনীর চমকটা ছিল অন্যখানে। যথারীতি পাহাড় থেকে ঘুরে আসার পর আমি একদিন গেছি কোলকাতা ময়দানে "তালতলা ইনষ্টিটিউটের" টেণ্টে আমার অগ্রজ, সুহৃদ তথা পর্বত পদযাত্রার অভিভাবকস্বরূপ প্রদীপ্ত চক্রবর্তী ওরফে দীপুদার ডাকে। চায়ের কাপ হাতে যখন আমার ভ্রমণ বৃত্তান্ত শেষ করলাম তখন দীপুদা বললেন, "আশিস, তুমি কি জানো যে পথে 'খাতি খাল' হয়ে তোমরা ফিরেছো সেটা এখন অপ্রচলিত।" আমি বললাম, " হ্যাঁ, খাতির চৌকিদার বলেছিল বটে। আগে নাকি পিন্ডারি যাবার ওটাই পথ ছিল।" দীপুদা আমার মুখের কথা কেড়ে নিয়ে বললেন, "হ্যাঁ, তখন ঢাকুরির পথে কেউ যেত না। তোমরা যেমন স্থানীয় চারজনকে খাতিখালের ওপরে দেখেছিলে, সেটাই ওদের স্বাভাবিক পথ ছিল বরাবরই। আর ১৮৯৩ সালে আচার্য্য জগদীশ চন্দ্র বসু ও তাঁর স্ত্রী অবলা বসু ঐ পথেই গিয়েছিলেন পিন্ডারি গ্লেসিয়ার দর্শনে আলমোড়া থেকে। আর তারই ফলশ্রুতি হলো আচার্য্য জগদীশ চন্দ্র বসুর শ্রেষ্ঠ রম্যরচনা "ভাগিরথীর উৎস সন্ধানে"। দীপুদা আরো জানালেন "ভাগিরথীর উৎস সন্ধানে" প্রথম প্রকাশিত হয় রামানন্দ চট্টোপাধ্যায় সম্পাদিত "দাসী" পত্রিকায় ১৮৯৫ সালে। জগদীশ চন্দ্র বসুর এই প্রথম রচনাই তাঁকে বাংলা সাহিত্যে লেখকের প্রতিষ্ঠা এনে দেয়। রচনাটি স্বয়ং রবীন্দ্রনাথ ঠাকুর কর্তৃক প্রশংসিত হয়।" আমি দীপুদার কথা শুনে বিস্ময়াবিষ্ট হয়ে যেন ফিরে গেছি ভাগিরথী তথা পিন্ডারি গঙ্গার উৎস মুখে অচেনা পথ ধরে এক চেনা গন্তব্যে।।

*****

Har Ki Doon

Asis Mukherjee

When I and Pradip Biswas, my friend cum colleague, were strolling in the market place of Dehradun for purchasing some essential items for our next few days trek to "Har Ki Doon", we came across two young guys from Kolkata, Prasanta alias Prasantada and Tarun, both employees of C. E. S. C. Kolkata. And in no time we were bonded into friendship when we came to know that our next day's venture was same to explore "Har Ki Doon". After procurement of our purchase we came back to our hotel and incidentally we all put up in the same hotel. So after repacking our goods we came to the lounge of the hotel to have tea and revise our plan of the tour.

Prasantada was the senior most in our group and a trained mountaineer also. So unanimously he was accepted as our leader by automatic choice. He was a member of "The Himalayan Club" of Kolkata. While I briefed our trekking programme, he told us that unlike ours they had a plan to cross "Jamuna Kanta", the pass on the Bandarpunch" range and descend via Jamunotri instead of coming down to the road head along the same route. They came prepared for that mission equipped with tent and other gears. So initially it was decided that we would go together up to Har Ki Doon, what was our primary objective. We came to our rooms after having our dinner retired to bed.

Next day morning we all got ready early in the morning and left the hotel to catch the bus for Netwar. At the bus stand when we booked our tickets we came to know that the bus was plying up to Mori, ten kilometers ahead of Netwar due to road damage between Netwar and Mori. We had to accept it. Earlier the bus was plying up to

Purola. Off late it was extended up to Taluka. But in Himalaya one must be prepared for any uncertainty. The bus started around eight thirty in the morning. We occupied our seats and put our rucksacks on the roof of the bus. Up to Purola the condition of the road was good. But despite that, the local bus took an unusually long time. We managed to have our lunch at Purola and again started for Mori. We observed the condition of the road was worse. By evening we reached Mori. We brought down our rucksacks from the roof of the bus and began to follow the local passengers heading for Netwar. It was around ten kilometers. Evening set in earlier in September. Before we reached Netwar it was dark enough to bring torches. We followed the men ahead and cautiously crossed the damaged portion of the road where a bridge was completely washed out. After a while we came to Netwar forest bungalow. Fortunately the caretaker of the bungalow was available at the bungalow and we could check in. He helped us a lot. He prepared tea for us and also cooked rice and we brought out our tinned chicken curry for our dinner. Around nine we slipped into our sleeping bags and in no time our fatigued body fell asleep.

Next morning when we woke up and came outside of the bungalow with our cups of tea we were awestruck at the beauty of the Netwar bungalow and its surroundings. The altitude of Netwar is 4600 feet. The deep gorge of the river Tonse was seen from the compound of the bungalow but the flow of the river was not visible from this place, only the gurgling sound of the river was heard. It was a confluence of the Rupin river coming from the right bank of the Tonse. We would go along the river Tonse towards its source. After breakfast we set out for Taluka, our today's destination via Sankri. In no time we entered into the forest of chestnuts, oaks and pines but the road up to Sankri was being built for bus, so the condition of the track was very good for trekkers. In near future the buses would ply up to

Taluka and then trekkers would certainly loose an opportunity to enjoy hiking through this dense forest. But now we're enjoying our journey through the dense forest. We could only have a glimpse of the monkeys and different varieties of birds. Though local people told us that bears and leopards were available in the forest but we were fortunate not to encounter any of them. Even though we were walking together. In two hours we reached Sankri. We came across a tea shop and the Supin river, another contributory, coming down to meet the Tonse. So we selected a nice place to have a break. After some time we again resumed our journey. Today's total distance is twenty kilometers. So far we had covered eight kilometers, less than half of the total journey. So we tried to cover the rest of the trek a bit faster so that we could reach Taluka and had our lunch over there. Because of the comfort of the route we reached, in the next three hours, Taluka at around 2 p.m. We checked in the forest bungalow and tried to prepare our lunch. The chaukidar also came forward to help us. Around 3 p.m. after having our lunch we felt comfortable and relaxed. On our way to Taluka we crossed two waterfalls which contributed their waters to the river Tonse. We walked along the left bank of Tonse and enjoyed our journey beside it all through. The Taluka bungalow offered us a wide space to enjoy our leasure at the balcony of the bungalow. The green fields of cultivation spread towards the bank of the river. The giant trees of the forest were set aside. We sat there for hours until sunset. Evening spread a curtain of darkness all over the valley and cold wind drove us inside the room. We observed that all the forest bungalows on our way were very good and well maintained. We had our booking from Kolkata through the Divisional Forest Office, Purola. We also noticed the board of the Forest Department on our way marking "Govind Pashu Vihar ". We are now in the reserve area of the forest. The altitude of Taluka is 6500 feet. So today we gained a height of around two thousand feet. So far we traversed through a good path because it was prepared to be motorable in the near future. But the more we marched ahead the more we entered into the deep forest. But from the compound of Taluka bungalow we could not even realise how wild and dense could it be. We also observed the planks of wood were flowing down the river. The natural transportation system of the wood cutters in the upper region of the forest. We had seen how the resins was extracted from the Pine trees in the forest. The forest here provided the bread and butter to the local people. With cups of tea we sat together in the room and I was telling my friends that we traversed through mythology and entered into the territory of the Kauravas of Mahabharata. The entire region along with the banks of the river Tonse was the kingdom of Kauravas and in many villages in the temples Duryodhan and Karna are still worshiped as local Gods. The story seemed unbelievable to my friends but I assured them that we would certainly come across on our way. Local people also believe that Pandava so went to their final departure from earth to heaven along this route because at the end of this route there stands the peaks of the Swargarohini means path to heaven and from that peaks descends the Jamdwar glacier which means the door to the next world after death. These mythological references give the trek a different dimension. Meanwhile the chaukidar of the bungalow prepared our dinner and called us. We noticed that the clock struck 8 p.m. So we moved for our dinner and called it a day.

Next morning we as usual started early after having our breakfast. Today's distance is around 14 k.m. but we have to traverse through dense forest along the foot track of the villagers. This is the third day of our trek. I was marching ahead followed by Pradip and then Prasantada and Tarun. The team automatically broke due to the different pace of the individuals. Sometimes the foot track came down to the level of the river bed, sometimes it was going up. At one point I noticed that the foot track was bifurcated and one track went to the right and upward direction. I paused for a while and decided to follow the left side narrow path through the dense forest along the course of the river leaving the right side a comparatively wider track. I thought twice before proceeding and put a cairn for my behinders so that they could follow the right direction. I was marching non-stop and sometimes I felt uncanny amidst the deep forest alone. Perhaps the feeling forced me to walk relentlessly. The track went through the course of Tonse. I am now confirmed that I have chosen the right track. After four hours and a half walking I came out of the jungle in an open field. I found green pasture of cultivated fields and my foot track went through the field of red and green. On one side of the field was the cultivation of Ramdana, the local name of a corn which was red and on the other side of the field was the cultivation of wheat which was green. I was lost for a while amidst the colours of life and the sign of human beings nearby. I stopped for some time after a long march. I found local women working in the fields and their houses nearby. I regained my energy after seeing them. I resumed my march with double energy and in no time I came to the village and found the forest bungalow. I noticed the signboard "Forest Bungalow, Oshla, elevation 8400 feet, Govind Pashu Vihar." I gradually entered the compound and put down my rucksack. But to my utter dismay I observed that the bungalow was preoccupied by a large group of people and porters. I could not understand who they were and when they had come because we didn't find anybody crossing us on the way. Meanwhile the chaukidar, Bhajan Sing appeared. He told me that a team from the Geological Survey of India had come yesterday. But he also assured me after seeing the boarding pass that there won't be any problem for us because the team consists of two officers and a number of porters and mules and they would move for Har ki Doon the next day. I was still hesitant. Meanwhile the two officers of G. S. I. came out and seeing me waiting there greeted me warmly and offered me a cup of tea also. In no time I got acquainted with them and felt relieved. I came to know that they had come here to conduct survey work at Har ki Doon area for a couple of days and after that they would go to Ruinsara Tal and survey there also. They also assured me that we won't face any problem on account of their presence. The Oslha forest bungalow was big enough with a covered balcony and a separate kitchen. It was situated on the left bank of the river Tonse and the name of the place was Seema and the village Oshla was clearly visible from here on the other side of the river. Now I became worried about my friends as the sun began to set in the west. Just by that time Pradip appeared followed by another aged gentleman but there was no sign of either Prasantada or Tarun. I immediately rushed to them and after a long time seeing me they also got relieved. I brought them on the balcony and served them with tea and biscuits. None of us had lunch today. So in this unknown route through dense forest everybody was fatigued. Then Pradip asked me about Prasantada and Tarun. When he came to know that they didn't turn up yet he also expressed his anxiety and told me that they might have lost the proper direction of the track in the forest. I asked him whether he noticed my direction mark at the diversion of the track, he then confirmed me nodding his head and added that they might have taken the right hand track without noticing the cairn made by me at that bifurcation point. Evening set in the valley, the surroundings sank into the darkness. I told Pradip to take a rest in the room. I managed to arrange tea in a flux and took some biscuits and set out for them with a torch. Within half a mile away I got them coming with leaden feet towards me with a torch in their hands. I rushed to them and they got back to life as soon as they heard my voice in the dark. I assured them that they had already arrived and told them to have tea and biscuits. After a little pause we resumed our journey with new energy. We stepped in the room at around seven in the evening. All of us were refreshed and had another round of tea. Now is the time to know what happened to them. Pradip's assumption was correct. They had taken the right hand track at the diversion point. Because that track was wider and more usable than the track leading towards Oshla and they reached the village Datmir. When they reached there they came to know from one of the villagers that they had reached the wrong destination. The villager told them to return and take the right hand narrow track along the river through the forest and he also assured Prasantada and Tarun that there won't be any problem to reach Oshla forest bungalow. So they had to trek more than four kilometers to reach here and when they came back again at the junction point they noticed my direction mark. Now everyone was settled and we had our dinner with the G. S. I. team and managed to sleep on our own matress at one corner of the room.

Next morning we woke up as usual and got prepared for our final destination. The G. S. I. Officers along with their porters, we four and the new gentleman who joined us yesterday all together it was a very big team in a word. All of us began to move after tea and breakfast. I was a bit worried about our accommodation for the night because I knew that Har Ki Doon bungalow had only one big room and it was not as big as that of Oslha. When I expressed this to my friends that somehow it would also be managed like last night and encouraged me to enjoy the journey and asked me, perhaps to divert my mind, about Oslha. We were walking together. Today's march is only ten kilometers but we have to climb around three thousand feet. We followed the banks of Tonse and came to the confluence of 'Har Ki Doon Nala' and 'Ruinsara Gad' the two rivulets. The 'Har Ki Doon Nala' is coming from the Jamdwar glacier and the 'Ruinsara Gad' is coming from the 'Ruinsara Tal' or lake situated at the bottom of the Bandarpunch Range. These two rivulets form here the river Tonse. I narrated the origin and description of the rivers to my friends. I added that 'Ruinsara Tal' is around fourteen kilometers from the Seema forest bungalow. It's a nice valley between Bandarpunch Range and Swargarohini Range and also the base camp for both the 'Swargarohini Peak' and the 'Kalanag' or the 'Black Peak'. There is a Col or Pass between these two ridges named 'Dhumdharkandi Pass' that connects the two valleys, the Tonse Valley and the ''Yamuna Valley'. We crossed the bridge on Tonse and left the confluence to the right bank of the Har Ki Doon Nala. A steep climb began. We came near the Oshla village. I insisted my friends to visit the temple of Duryodhan in the village. Everyone of us saw for the first time a temple of the local God in this region and got a touch of the local culture. The temple was completely made of wood and both the craftsmanship and the design were very attractive. We came back to our track leading to Har Ki Doon. The forest of the giant trees were left behind. Only bush and birch trees were seen now. Everyone was moving at one's own pace. The trail to Ruinsara Tal was visible now from here on the other bank of the river Tonse. The two ranges of Mount Swargarohini and Bandarpunch were also visible. We were marching slowly but steadily on our way. There was no flat land, no village ahead, so no tea shop to rest for a while, we all walked and walked relentlessly. We all were walking together. At length we realised that there was no steep ascent, the track was almost flat, stretched through the grassland. We all were fatigued and paused for a while. I told my friends that J. T. M. Gibson visited the valley in 1948 and in his write-up published in the Himalayan Journal in 1954, he introduced this marvelous valley to trekkers and mountain lovers of the world. We came up on the grassland and noticed a number of colourful tents on the bank of the river. A group of foreigners came to enjoy the beauty of the place. The

Swargarohini stood tall on the other bank of the river and a stream was coming from Jamdwar glacier pouring its water into the Har Ki Doon Nala and another stream, named Morinda was coming from left the Borasu Pass, which connected the Himachal Pradesh and the Uttarakhand. Mr. Gibson came from that side crossing the Borasu Pass. Later he came here on an expedition to Swargarohini and Black Peak with a group of students. When we arrived at the Har Ki Doon bungalow we found that the G. S. I. team had already arrived there. This bungalow was comparatively small containing one big room and below one separate kitchen. We were welcomed by the G. S. I. team and we unleashed our rucksacks and took everyone a cup of tea. Today we prepared our food with the help of their cook. But we all had our lunch together. After lunch we came out of the bungalow for a stroll around. We first walked along the stream coming from Borasu Pass. Tomorrow we shall go to the Jamdwar glacier. The glacier that comes down from Swargarohini. The name of the glacier is aptly given. Jamdwar means the gateway to the next world after death and Swargarohini means path to heaven. A silver thread like stream is coming down from the Jamdwar glacier through the picturesque valley at the foot of Swargarohini and pouring its water into the stream that coming from Borasu Pass and both the streams together form the Har Ki Doon Nala which again after meeting with the stream of the Ruinsara Gad at Oshla form the Har Ki Doon Nala. Har Ki Doon means the abode of Lord Shiva. In every sphere of the locality and life here there is a mythological references to Mahabharata. We came back to the bungalow. We were having a discussion with the G. S. I. officers. They would stay here for a week and conduct their survey work around both the regions. Tomorrow we shall go to the Jamdwar glacier along the stream as far as we can go and then we shall go back to Oslha.

So after dinner we went to the kitchen and laid our matress and sleeping bags. Here we were five trekkers now. Rest of all stayed at the bungalow. In the morning when I woke up at the call of a porter I was awestruck at the first sight of the Swargarohini visible from my bed through the open doors just a few kilometers away. The rays of the morning sun were appearing behind it and black and snow white Swargarohini standing in front of me as if inviting me to the abode of God. I can never forget that moment in my life even after seeing many a sunrise either at the mountain or at the sea. I woke up at my bed and with the cup of tea enjoyed the beauty of the Har Ki Doon valley through the open door. After two three sips of tea the trance was over and I left my bed and packed up. In less than an hour we got ready and after another round of tea and biscuits set out for Jamdwar glacier. It's a flat trail and on our right side the Har Ki Doon Nala was flowing through the meadow silently and on its other bank stood the Swargarohini like a huge wall. This side of the Swargarohini is the Har Ki Doon valley and the other side of it is the Ruinsara Gad. We walked slowly towards Jamdwar glacier and gradually appeared at the morain of the glacier and saw the ice fall came down from Swargarohini and water was gushing out from the mouth of the glacier. We paused there for some time and took some snaps and returned. The valley, the mountain, the mythological references all were filled in the books and volumes of my memory but above all the most vivid picture was the dawn at Swargarohini. We returned from the Jamdwar glacier murmuring the song of Bob Dylan "Knock, Knock, Knocking on Heaven's Door...".

We came back to Har Ki Doon bungalow and had our lunch over there with the G. S. I. officers and without wasting time bade goodbye to our host the G. S. I. team and set out for Oshla. Still ten kilometers we had to trek and it's midday now. But the trail was good and it was descending from 11,200 feet to 8400 feet. So we all comfortably reached the Seema forest bungalow at around 4 p.m. We checked in and asked Bhajan Sing, the chaukidar, to prepare tea for us. After tea break we all assembled at the balcony of the bungalow and exchanged our experiences and discussed our next day's plan. So far everything happened so smoothly that we didn't face any hazard in our trek.

Next morning we set out after breakfast. Today our four men team will break. Prasantada and Tarun will head for Jamuna Kanta, the pass over Bandarpunch Range and go via Jamunotri, the source of the Jamuna river and Pradip and myself and the aged gentleman from Kolkata will go for Taluka. We all started together and after coming a furlong they took the trail to Jamuna Kanta accompanied by a local guide and we wished them good luck and took our trail towards Taluka. In four hours and a half we reached Taluka bungalow. The chaukidar welcomed us and opened the doors. We checked in and asked him for tea and lunch. Sitting at the balcony of the bungalow we recapitulated our past few days' trek. In the evening we came inside the room and helped the chaukidar to prepare our dinner.

Early in the morning we set out after having a cup of tea only. Today's is a long march of twenty kilometers. We had planned to have some food on the way. We tried to speed up from the beginning so that we could reach Netwar comfortably before evening. On the way we stopped at a shop for some food. We reached Netwar bungalow in the afternoon. Now on our return journey we felt the bungalow and the chaukidar very familiar. As we checked in the chaukidar prepared tea for us. We asked him to prepare our dinner also. We got together at the balcony of the bungalow and went on gossiping until evening fell. Tomorrow is the last leg of our trek. Prasantada and Tarun might have reached Jamunotri today. So they also will discend tomorrow to reach the roed head. They had to spend one night in the tent on their way. Next day morning we also started early so that we could catch the bus for Dehradun from Mori. On our way we again crossed the broken road and in the daylight we saw that it was completely washed out in the stream. On the very first day of our trek we could not realise the gravity of the damage. But now in the daylight it was frightening. Nevertheless we crossed it safely along with other villagers and appeared at the bus stand. Fortunately we got the bus also for Dehradun. In the trek in Himalaya, I've observed that if fortune gives you a stand you can overcome any odd situation. By grace of the God 'Har' or 'Mahadev', this time also we could complete our trek safely and came back from 'Jamdwar' or 'Heaven's Door'.

*****